CANTERBURY STUDIES
IN ANGLICANISM

Calling on the Spirit in Unsettling Times

CANTERBURY STUDIES
IN ANGLICANISM
Series Editors: Martyn Percy and Ian Markham

Calling on the Spirit in Unsettling Times

Anglican Present and Future

L. William Countryman

Morehouse Publishing
NEW YORK · HARRISBURG · DENVER

Morehouse Publishing
4775 Linglestown Road, Harrisburg, PA 17112

Morehouse Publishing
445 Fifth Avenue, New York, NY 10016

Morehouse Publishing is an imprint of
Church Publishing Incorporated.
www.churchpublishing.org

Cover design by Laurie Klein Westhafer
Typeset by Vicki K. Black

Library of Congress Cataloging-in-Publication Data
   Countryman, Louis William, 1941–
   Calling on the Spirit in unsettling times / L. William Countryman.
      p.   cm. — (Canterbury studies in Anglicanism)
   Includes bibliographical references.
   ISBN 978-0-8192-2770-6 (pbk.) — ISBN 978-0-8192-2771-3 (ebook)
   1. Anglican Communion—History—21st century. 2. Church renewal—Anglican Communion. I. Title.

   BX5005.C68 2012
   262'.03—dc23
                                                    2011045362

Printed in the United States of America

10   9   8   7   6   5   4   3   2   1

IN MEMORY OF M. R. RITLEY,
*who was always open
to the Spirit's leading*

CONTENTS

ACKNOWLEDGMENTS

My thanks to those who first prompted me to put together my thoughts on these matters and present them as lectures in 2010:

To the Reverend Geoff Butcher and the clergy and people of Christ Church Cathedral, Nashville, Tennessee, who heard the first version of chapters three and four.

To my Australian hosts, particularly the Reverend Matthew Healy and the Society of Catholic Priests, the Right Reverend John Parkes, Bishop of Wangaratta, and the Reverend Rob Whalley, who persuaded me to undertake a speaking trip there. My thanks also to the many others in Australia who welcomed me and fostered my work there and made the communion of saints come alive in new ways for me—more names than I have space to list here.

To the people of Good Shepherd Episcopal Church in Berkeley, California, who listened to several of the lectures and made helpful suggestions. Thanks particularly to Paula White, who suggested valuable changes in chapter two.

My thanks also to those who read the manuscript in various stages of revision and encouraged me to move toward publication: my sister Betty Keely, Davis Perkins at Morehouse Publishing, and Christine Smith at Canterbury Press.

FOREWORD TO THE SERIES

by the Archbishop of Canterbury

The question "What is the real identity of Anglicanism?" has become more pressing and more complex than ever before in the last decade or so, ecumenically as well as internally. Is the Anglican identity a matter of firm Reformed or Calvinist principle, resting its authoritative appeal on a conviction about the sovereignty and all-sufficiency of Scripture interpreted literally? Is it a form of non-papal Catholicism, strongly focused on sacramental and ministerial continuity, valuing the heritage not only of primitive Christianity but also of mediaeval and even post-Reformation Catholic practice and devotion? Is it an essentially indeterminate Christian culture, particularly well-adapted to the diversity of national and local sympathies and habits? Is the whole idea of an "ism" misplaced here?

Each of these models has its defenders across the Communion; and each has some pretty immediate consequences for the polity and politics of the global Anglican family. Some long for a much more elaborately confessional model than has generally been the case—the sort of model that those who defined the boundaries of the Church of England in the sixteenth century were very wary of. Some are happy with the idea of the Communion becoming a federation of local bodies with perhaps, in the long run, quite markedly diverging theologies and disciplines. The disagreements over the ordination of women and the Church's response to lesbian and gay people have raised basic issues around the liberty of local churches to decide what are thought by many to be secondary matters; the problem then being that not everyone agrees that they are secondary. The question of identity is inseparable from the question of unity: to recognize another community as essentially the same, whatever divergences there may be in language and practice, is necessary for any unity that is more than formal—for a unity that issues in vigorous evangelism and consistent "diaconal" service to the world.

And this means in turn that questions about Anglican identity will inevitably become questions about the very nature of the Church—and thus the nature of revelation and incarnation and the character of God's activity. I believe it is generally a piece of deplorably overheated rhetoric to describe those holding different views around the kind of questions I have mentioned as being adherents of "different religions"; but there is an uncomfortable sense in which this exaggeration reminds us that the line between primary and secondary issues is not self-evidently clear—or at least that what we say about apparently secondary matters may reveal something about our primary commitments.

The long and short of it is that we should be cautious of saying of this or that development or practice "It isn't Anglican," as if that settled the matter. One of the first tasks we need to pursue in the current climate is simply to look at what Anglicans say and do. We need to watch Anglicans worshipping, constructing patterns for decision-making and administration, arguing over a variety of moral issues (not only sexuality), engaging in spiritual direction and the practices of private prayer. Without this, we shan't be in a good position to assess whether it's the same religion; and we are very likely to be assuming that what we take for granted is the norm for a whole church or family of churches.

The books in this series are attempts to do some of this "watching"—not approaching the question of identity in the abstract but trying to discern how Anglicans identify themselves in their actual life together, locally and globally. I'd like to think that they might challenge some of the more unhelpful clichés that can be thrown around in debate, the stereotypes used by both Global South and Global North about each other. If it is true that—as I have sometimes argued in other places—true interfaith dialogue only begins as you watch the other when their faces are turned to God, this must be true a fortiori in the Christian context. And I hope that some of these essays will allow a bit of that sort of watching. If they do, they will have helped us turn away from the lethal temptation to talk always about others when our backs are turned to them (and to God).

We all know that simply mapping the plurality of what Anglicans do is not going to answer the basic question, of course. But it is a necessary discipline for our spiritual health. It is in the light of this that we can begin to think through the broader theological issues. Let's say for the sake of argument that church communities in diverse contexts with diverse convictions about some of the major issues of the day do as a matter of bare fact manage to acknowledge each other as Anglican disciples of Jesus Christ to the extent that they are able to share some resources in theological training and diaconal service: the task then is to try and tease out what—as a matter of bare fact—makes them recognizable to each other. Not yet quite theology, but a move towards it, and above all a move away from mythologies and projections.

If I had to sum up some of my own convictions about Anglican identity, I should, I think, have to begin with the fact that, at the beginning of the English Reformation, there was a widespread agreement that Catholic unity was secured not by any external structures alone but by the faithful ministration of Word and Sacrament—"faithful" in the sense of unadulterated by mediaeval agendas about supernatural priestly power or by the freedom of a hierarchical Church to add new doctrinal refinements to the deposit of faith. Yet as this evolved a little further, the Reformers in Britain turned away from a second-generation Calvinism which would have alarmed Calvin himself and which argued for a wholly literal application of biblical law to the present times and the exclusion from church practice of anything not contained in the plain words of Scripture. Gradually the significance of a continuous ministry in the historic style came more into focus as a vehicle of mutual recognition, eventually becoming the straightforward appeal to apostolic episcopal succession often thought to be a central characteristic of the Anglican tradition.

The blend of concern for ordered ministry (and thus ordered worship), freedom from an uncritical affirmation of hierarchical ecclesiastical authority, with the appeal to Scripture at the heart of this, and the rooted belief that the forms of common worship were the most important clues about what was held to be recognizably orthodox teaching—this blend or fusion came to define the Anglican ethos in a growing diversity of cultural contexts. Catholic, yes, in the sense of seeing the Church today as responsible to its history and to the gifts of God in the past, even those gifts given to people who have to be seen as in some ways in error. Reformed, yes, in the sense that the principle remains of subjecting the state of the Church at any given moment to the judgement of Scripture—though not necessarily therefore imagining that Scripture alone offers the answer to every contemporary question. And running through the treatment of these issues, a further assumption that renewal in Christ does not abolish but fulfils the long-frustrated capacities of human beings: that we are set free to sense and to think the texture of God's Wisdom in the whole of creation and at the same time to see how it is itself brought to fulfilment in the cross of Jesus.

This is the kind of definition that a sympathetic reading of the first two Anglican centuries might suggest. It certainly has implications for where we find the centre for such a definition in our own day. But the point is that it is a historical argument, not one from first principles; or rather, the principles emerge as the history is traced. Once again, it is about careful watching—not as an excuse for failing to look for a real theological centre but as a discipline of discerning the gifts that have actually been given to us as Anglicans.

Not many, I suspect, would seriously want to argue that the Anglican identity can be talked about without reference to Catholic creeds and ministry, or to think that a "family" of churches can be spoken of without spelling out at least the essential family resemblances in terms of what Christ has uniquely done and what Christ continues to do in his Body through Word and Sacrament. But to understand how this does and does not, can and cannot, work, we need the kind of exact and imaginative study that this series offers us. I hope that many readers will take the trouble to work with the grain of such investigations, so that our life in the Communion (and in communion itself in its fullest sense, the communion of the Holy Spirit) will be enriched as well as calmed, and challenged as well as reinforced.

+ *Rowan Cantuar:*
from Lambeth Palace, Advent 2009

PREFACE

The last few decades have been difficult for Anglicans, as we find ourselves being pulled apart by disagreements over issues of gender and sexuality. In some ways, these tensions reflect deep disagreements about authority for doctrine and methods of theological reasoning. In other respects, they are deeply entangled with demographic and political shifts. In some places, these disagreements have produced varying degrees of schism; in others, they threaten to do so in the near future.

For Anglicans in the West (the only part of the world of which I can speak from personal experience) these internal conflicts coincide with cultural changes that have made Christianity in general (or, at least, its classical representations in the Anglican, Roman Catholic, and "mainline" Protestant traditions) seem increasingly irrelevant to large numbers of people. Even those who respect religion are sometimes suspicious of "church." Travel and cultural institutions such as art museums have taken religion's place as inspiration for many educated people, while groups of professional colleagues or associations based on shared interests fill the place of church communities.

Some suggest that this is part of a transition from a "modern" to a "postmodern" world. In the modern world, Christianity might be honored or attacked, but it was at least worth noticing because it was part of an inherited cultural core in the West. In the postmodern world, there is less of a common, inherited center of any kind, and correspondingly less presupposition that the church is worth bothering about.

The premise of this book is that our current troubles call Anglicans to a reappraisal of who we are in the world and to new hope. They are not simply a problem inflicted from without, but a challenge from the Holy Spirit, pressing us to reexamine the character of our faith and life, to think anew about what in our heritage we must hang onto and where we must seek new ways of living and communicating the good news.

The Holy Spirit is pressing us to reflect on the quality of the faith, hope, and love that we share and the character of our life together in the Anglican Communion. She has played a role in creating our current troubles and she will be the prime mover in inspiring and enabling the reconstruction of our life in the years to come. This will not involve the rejection of what has been central to our faith, but it will demand its renewal and transformation.

Since it is impossible to imagine that anyone would write a book such as this without a personal stake or perspective in addressing our present troubles, the reader might wish to know a little something right from the start about where the author locates himself in contemporary Anglicanism. I am an American and a priest of the Episcopal Church. I am Professor Emeritus of Biblical Studies at the Church Divinity School of the Pacific in Berkeley, California, and a poet as well as a scholar of scripture and spirituality. While I have never been comfortable about defining myself in terms of church politics, I find myself most at ease and experience the least need to explain my presuppositions among those Anglicans called "affirming" or "liberal" catholics. The label implies both a strong attachment to tradition and a willingness to revisit and rethink it when it threatens to become a vehicle of something other than the good news of Jesus Christ. I will return to the larger question of "intra-Anglican" identities in chapter five.

My intention is not to vindicate any one position within Anglicanism or to identify a core Anglicanism, but to ask how all aspects of our heritage may participate in a future that the Spirit is even now in the process of creating. We cannot expect to know this future in detail before we arrive there. We will come to know it in the creation of it. It will not, however, be discontinuous with our past. In the past, we have lived by the gifts of God; the future, too, depends on these gifts.

1

CALLING ON THE SPIRIT
IN UNSETTLING TIMES

Anglican reformers of the sixteenth century made an unusual decision when they chose to focus and shape our common faith through public prayer. It was not without controversy. Many Puritans objected vehemently to the *Book of Common Prayer* (*BCP*) on the grounds that it embodied a cold formalism and virtually constituted a third testament of scripture.[1] And even the most faithful of Anglicans have sometimes found it constricting or perhaps even misleading in its characterization of human life and Christian faith.

But whatever its merits or inadequacies and however much it has been revised over the centuries, the *Book of Common Prayer* established one very important point. The first thing Anglicans do together, in principle, is not to theologize, but to pray. Accordingly, each chapter of this book will begin with prayer and with some reflection on that prayer. Some of the prayers will come from the *BCP*. But some will come from another source, an unquestionably orthodox Anglican laywoman of the late nineteenth century, known to us primarily as a poet: Christina Rossetti.

Late in life, she wrote a commentary on the Revelation to John, published just two years before her death. It combines a wide array of writings: interpretive materials drawn from the biblical scholars of the day, prose reflections on the spiritual meaning of the text, expostulations, prayers, and some splendid poetry. Here is one of the prayers:

O God, only Good, think upon Thy congregation whom Thou hast purchased and redeemed of old. Rule all hearts by Thy Most Holy Spirit; that humbly we may worship Thee, and truthfully confess Thee, owning ourselves unprofitable servants, and in honour preferring one another. To the praise of our Lord Jesus Christ. Amen.[2]

Rossetti lived in a time not unlike ours, when the church seemed threatened by indifference without and conflict within. It was being pushed aside by scientific positivism and the industrial age's fixation on profit. It was also riven from within by disputes between Anglo-Catholics and Evangelicals and suffered significant losses on the Anglo-Catholic side from conversions to Roman Catholicism. Even though her prayer is that of an individual, she was formed by the church's common prayer; and she implicitly invited her readers to pray with her. It is a prayer in and on behalf of the church.

The central petition is "Rule all hearts by Thy Most Holy Spirit." Anglicans do not usually start with the Holy Spirit—after all, the Spirit is hard to say much about. We can think of God the Father in concrete terms as Creator of the world. We turn to the Gospels for the still more concrete image of Jesus, the Incarnate Word. With the Spirit, we are apt to lose our bearings, our footing, our certainties. "The wind (*pneuma,* spirit) blows where it chooses, and you hear the sound of it, but you do not know where it comes from or where it goes" (John 3:8).

Those words come from Jesus' conversation with Nicodemus, early in John's Gospel, where he is telling Nicodemus that he has to be born "over again" or "from above" of the Spirit. And Nicodemus cannot understand what Jesus is getting at, though he remains fascinated by Jesus' teaching. Things get no easier at the end of John's Gospel, when Jesus returns to the subject of the Spirit. In the discourse where he bids farewell to his disciples, he declares, "I will ask the Father, and he will give you another Advocate, to be with you forever. This is the Spirit of truth, whom the world cannot receive, because it neither sees him nor knows him. You know him, because he abides with you, and he will be in you"

(14:16–17). And a little later: "The Advocate, the Holy Spirit, whom the Father will send in my name, will teach you everything, and remind you of all that I have said to you" (14:26). And again, "When the Spirit of truth comes, he will guide you into all the truth; for he will not speak on his own, but will speak whatever he hears, and he will declare to you the things that are to come" (16:13).[3]

So here is the Spirit present at our beginning as confused and uncertain disciples. The Spirit acts on us in the baptism of new birth. The Spirit is in us and with us as we seek to understand Jesus' meaning, as we look into an uncertain future, as we ask how we are to be faithful while moving forward into a time that seems less friendly than we had expected. And Jesus says to the disciples—that is, to us—"I understand your anxiety; I sympathize with it. But you won't need my concrete, personal guidance now. The Spirit will be *in* you. I and my Father will put the Spirit in you, and we will be with you in and through the Spirit."

It doesn't make matters any easier, does it? No. Nor is that the point, of course. The Spirit, by definition, is the One whom we cannot get the hang of, whom we cannot even pretend to be in control of, the One who will always outfox us and surprise us, particularly at the moments when we feel most confident. The Spirit can be comforting. The Spirit can also be alarming and unsettling. Either way, the Spirit is always beyond our grasp.

Calling on the Spirit

"Rule all hearts by Thy Most Holy Spirit." Rossetti chose her words with care. She was a brilliant poet, who is now coming back into critical esteem after being ignored for about a century. (Some thought she should be poet laureate after the death of Tennyson, but a woman as laureate was too much for that era.) And she was a devout Anglo-Catholic, a faith she shared with her sister, who joined one of the revived religious orders for women. She lived through a period of intra-church conflict not unlike ours. Indeed, her parish priest—William Dodsworth—was one of the Anglo-Catholic leaders who seceded to Rome. Rossetti was not tempted to follow. Her father had been forced to flee Italy for his liberal politics, and she harbored no romanticism about the papacy. She firmly opposed secession in that direction.[4]

She also recognized the more hidden spiritual dangers of such a time of trouble. She prays—we pray with her—that, by the gift of the Spirit, we may "humbly worship" God. To worship humbly may sound like a matter of self-abasement. But, no, that's not it. Worship is a celebration of God's goodness, which is beyond anything we can imagine or desire. There may be room in it for noticing that we do not measure up so well ourselves—but not very much room. We do not occupy center stage here; our failings are just not that interesting. To worship means to rejoice in the beauty of the Lover who has come seeking us as beloved, however unworthy we may be.

To worship *humbly* means to set aside our own ambitions and anxieties long enough to celebrate God our Lover, God who is only Good. The church has repeatedly tried to portray itself as something more official and authoritative than God's beloved—perhaps God's press secretary or police officer. Perhaps God's substitute teacher. Certainly, God's vicar. Christians have often acted as if we alone have God's ear. We exclude from God's confidence not only people of other faiths, but also other Christians who disagree with us. Rossetti did not fall into this trap. Even though she disagreed strongly with the Anglo-Catholic leaders who crossed the Tiber, she never, as far as I can tell, wrote anybody off because of such disagreements. Her generous and loving sonnet on the death of Cardinal Newman asserts that he "chose love not in the shallows but the deep" and concludes:

> Thy best has done its best, thy worst its worst;
> Thy best its best, please God, thy best its best.[5]

The repetition of that last phrase acknowledges her doubts about his course of action and yet leaves no room for anger or rejection, only for the praise of love and faithfulness. Her prayer that the Spirit would enable us to worship *humbly* was no formality. She knew what she was asking for.

She also asked—we ask with her—that we might *truthfully confess* the God who is only Good. Well, yes, the Spirit is certainly not going to get involved in any form of confession that is less than truthful. The Spirit Jesus left with us is the Spirit of Truth. To confess God means to tell of God's goodness. And that does not mean doing a public relations job for God. In the Book of Job, Job insists that God has punished him even though he was not at fault. Job's three pious comforters try to defend God: "Job, you know you're in the wrong. Go ahead and confess your sinfulness. God will forgive you and make everything right again." But at the end of the book, God says to them, "You have not spoken of me what is right, as my servant Job has done" (42:8). They thought it was better to fudge the truth a bit so as to make God look better, but God does not want that. God wants us to be honest about our world, our experience, our uncertainties, even our lack of perfect comprehension. Only by truth, only by shunning all lies and cover-ups, can we truthfully confess the True God.

And finally, Rossetti concludes with a double request in this prayer: that we may worship and confess God while "owning ourselves unprofitable servants, and in honour preferring one another." In more prosaic terms, it means that we admit that we have not done so well ourselves and we give each other some respect. The goal of the Christian life is not to claim any kind of certainty or perfection for ourselves. The goal is to work toward a community in which we can praise one another, accepting one another's gifts with joy and generosity. That is a vision of church that is worth praying for, worth embracing, worth trying to live into. And it is a vision of the church that, I would imagine, every one of us has in fact experienced as reality at some time or other. We have probably experienced some other, less attractive realities of church, too. I don't deny that. But we know what the church *can* be when it is ruled by the Holy Spirit. There is no room in it for fraud or arrogance. It is a community of people who can worship humbly and confess truthfully and who do not feel the need to make much of themselves but who are genuinely, deeply delighted by one another's gifts. It is the Spirit who makes this possible.

Our unsettled times

The church, poised in an unsettled state between past and future, is the central topic of this book. But I begin with the Spirit, even though I suspect we would all rather start from some more definite anchorage, a set of eternal and unambiguous verities, a boundary marker that we can keep coming back to. And yet, this seems the right place, especially in the way Rossetti phrases it for us. When we find ourselves in difficult times, it will actually be helpful to take as our starting point one who is beyond our grasp and is nonetheless our Advocate and guide, our reminder of Jesus and the guardian of honesty and integrity. We do not, after all, understand our current position. Well, some of us think we do, but there is no clear evidence that any of our internal Anglican parties actually possesses the keys to the future, even if some of them claim to. What we need, rather, is to find a new sense of possibility and hope—and, at the same time, to renew our sense of humble worship, truthful confession, and love and respect for one another. Anglicans are not alone in this. Christians of all sorts find themselves right now confronting times of change, flux, perhaps threat.

The threats and challenges are different in different parts of the world. In many countries right now it is dangerous to be a Christian. Throughout the world, Christians suffer along with everyone else the consequences of natural and human-caused disasters, of political upheaval, of dislocated economies. If Anglicans who live in Western countries are somewhat better cushioned against their ill-effects, we are not immune; and the problems that do not confront us directly still touch us through people who are sisters and brothers in Christ even if we do not know them personally.

And Anglicans in the West face our own challenges. Some are demographic in character. Australia and North America, for example, both experience ongoing urbanization and the attendant draining of people away from more rural areas. This threatens the continued existence of parishes and dioceses in such regions. In one rural American diocese the new bishop is also serving as rector of one of the larger parishes. This represents a return to an older pattern of episcopal organization in the United States, and it may prove an excellent solution. But it also raises the question of whether this diocese, located in the wheat-and-cattle country of the High Plains, will need to consider reuniting with its parent Diocese of Kansas, which covers the more urban eastern part of the state. Similar challenges face rural dioceses in Canada, Australia, Ireland, and Great Britain.

In the cities, too, the shifting of ethnic groups and the aging of populations create challenges. The population of California, where I live, is becoming less and less "Anglo" and Black and more and more Hispanic and Asian. A neighborhood church may easily find itself in the midst of a new population with no history of an Anglican connection. I attend a small church in Berkeley, California, that has just celebrated its one hundred thirty-third birthday. Over that time, the congregation has waxed and waned and changed in ethnic composition several times. And it is no closer to assured stability today than when it was first founded.

There are also cultural shifts, including increased indifference toward the church on the part of many. The United States is unusual among industrialized nations in having a high percentage of church members. Still, recent studies indicate that the "religiously unaffiliated" is the most rapidly growing group. Even the Southern Baptists, who pride themselves on evangelism, seem to be shrinking. In other words, indifference (and sometimes hostility) toward the church seems to be more widespread. People doubt that religious communities have much of value to contribute to human life. This challenges us both practically and personally: Why is our faith and our connection with the church important for us? Why do other people just not "get" it? And what do words like "humble worship" and "truthful confession" mean as we get shoved around by such cultural shifts?[6]

Our world is also caught up in political tensions that are difficult to understand and impossible to control. The uprisings of 2011 in North Africa and the Middle East underscore the fact that even laudable movements like the drive toward freedom and democracy can produce new uncertainties and dangers. We confront war and terrorism, vast discrepancies of wealth, chaotic markets, oppressive governments, overpopulation, mass movements of population, threats of food shortages, and the overarching issue of the planet's health and well-being. Neither the church nor the "secular" culture seems able to move all these mountains, despite sometimes heroic efforts to provide relief. But that does not leave us free to ignore them either. Indeed, religion gets blamed for some of our problems, notably conflicts with an overtly religious element and issues of the environment, where Christianity is widely perceived as manifesting a certain indifference toward the natural world.

On top of these broad cultural shifts, there are problems created by the churches themselves—most obviously the newly revealed stories of malfeasance and abuse, particularly abuse of children. At one time—not so very long ago—these things might have been hushed up with the help of the press and even the police. That is no longer the case. And if we are tempted to rue that shift, we had better remember again that the Advocate Jesus promised us is called "the Spirit of Truth." Probably the Spirit is herself involved in pushing the church into a new openness, telling us that we cannot worship humbly or confess truthfully if we do not attend to the abuse and lies that sometimes afflict our own life together. What we refused to deal with forthrightly, she will drag right out into the open.

Then, of course, there is the open conflict within churches, including Anglican churches, over gender issues—primarily ordination of women and equality for lesbian/gay/bisexual/transgendered people. One might wonder at times whether the church is melting away around us. And we might well think so if we only read the newspapers and did not actually go to church and see, for the most part, people worshiping together as before. Even apart from the threat to our life together, however, the publicity attending these disagreements has left many people wondering whether the church can be taken seriously. Conservatives think it has sold out to the liberals. Liberals think it has sold out to the conservatives. Centrists invoke a plague on both their houses. If one relied on news reports alone, it would seem that the church is consumed with conflict and dissatisfaction.

None of this, of course, is news to the reader of this book. My purpose in reciting it is not to inform anyone, but to specify the context for the thinking and praying in which I hope we can join. This is the unsettled and unsettling context in which we live right now as faithful people, the context in which we *are* the church—and therefore it is also the context in which the Spirit is at work.

The living Spirit

We have Jesus' assurance that the Spirit does not abandon us. No matter how difficult she may be to discern at any given moment, the Spirit is always at work among us and in the world around us. Nothing can keep her out. This does not mean that people are always responding positively or cooperating. Neither in the church nor in the world can we assume that; both alike are capable of wrongdoing, even of grave evil.

But the Spirit is still at work, which means that the task before us is, humbly and hopefully, to seek out the traces of that work, to decipher the directions the Spirit is pointing us. Where then do we begin to look? What work do we expect the Spirit to be doing? We have some traditional answers—and they are good ones: we expect the Spirit to be active in the sacramental life of the church, in the reading of the scriptures, in the communion of saints of which we are a part, and in the life of prayer and reflection that we refer to as "spirituality." These experiences of the Spirit's power have shaped us over our lifetimes and they have shaped Anglicanism over the centuries. They are essential to our identity as Christian and Anglican people, and we shall return to them in chapters three and four.

And if we remember that the Giver is greater than the gift, we shall not make the mistake of supposing that these gifts are rigidly fixed—beyond reinterpreting or reimagining as the Spirit takes up her work in new circumstances. It takes nothing away from the power and virtue of the sacraments or scripture to admit that they stand on a level less authoritative, less decisive, less life-giving than the Spirit herself. There is a name in scripture for the error that confuses the gift with the giver. It is called "idolatry." And it continues to be, as it has

9

always been, one of the critical temptations for religious folk. We need to learn how to prize and honor the gifts we have received from the Spirit, while also recognizing that the Spirit has not composed the existing patterns of church life and theology as a tidy and inalterable package for all time. Then we shall be able to find in our heritage resources for the new creative endeavors necessary in our time and place. We can learn how to honor our inheritance without mistaking it for God.

In addition to the gifts we have inherited, the Spirit continues to work among us in less codified ways. Above all, the Spirit *liberates.* The earliest Christians experienced their conversion as a liberation from the narrow expectations that had hedged them in before. They heard the gospel telling them that God truly and deeply cares about human beings. God is not just the universal emperor, remote and withdrawn and immensely powerful. God comes close to us, seeking out people to engage with God's goodness, to receive God's gifts and share them with others. This is the meaning of the *charismata,* the gifts of the Spirit that have always been a part of Christian faith and life. They take different forms in different times and places, but they are always gifts of liberation, freeing us to deal with our world and its challenges because we know that God is actively involved in the process.

Sometimes the liberation is quite personal in form. From earliest times, for example, some Christians experienced the phenomenon of speaking in tongues. This gift, it seems, allows some people to surrender themselves to God in a way that was not otherwise possible for them. (I am basing this description on what I have heard from people who have experienced it. I have experienced such liberation, too, though not in the form of this particular charisma.) This sort of personal liberation is important, but it is not the whole story. Paul could list, alongside it and even in preference to it, such gifts as prophetic insight, wisdom, knowledge, the ability to share wealth instead of being enslaved to it, and the power to heal or to lead (1 Cor. 12:1–14:19)—gifts that overflow the realm of the personal into that of the community.

St. Francis's love affair with Sister Poverty would be such a gift. His passionate embrace of weakness and dependency freed him from the preoccupation with status and wealth that had characterized him as a youth; it opened him to the leading of the Spirit in relating to the world around him. Even his asceticism was not a rejection of the created world. He loved the whole creation. He saw God at work in it. His embrace of poverty was rather a way of seeing the world anew in the light of the Spirit and becoming free of anxiety and stepping into the work prepared for him. The gifts he received have proven to be so contagious that they still enliven the faith of multitudes.

The Spirit's gifts to us may be as personal and fleeting as the touch of peace that even the most anxious will sometimes feel upon entering a church; the sense of God's presence when you come across running water in an arid place or catch a glimpse of the sea from a forested hill; or the sense of exaltation that comes with hearing a Bach fugue. Private as such experiences seem, however, they do not stop with the individual recipient. They have the potential to transform us and, through us, to reach out into the world around us. Indeed, all the gifts of the Spirit ultimately direct us toward the larger community and the sharing of the gift.

The Spirit is at work in us and with us. She has the power to know us from within—better than we know ourselves. Every time you understand and overcome your self-deceptions, it is the Spirit. Every time you learn to hope again or find the power to move toward God, it is the Spirit. Whether this happens in private, as when we enter the innermost shrine of the heart, or whether it happens in the company of others, through words spoken by trusted advisors, through the word of scripture, through the sacraments and the experience of common prayer, makes no difference. And then you find you have something of grace to offer others.

All this sounds very miscellaneous. Yes, exactly. My examples come from all over the map, because that is where the Spirit finds us. There is no corner of human life that the Spirit has not reached ahead of us, where she is not waiting to surprise us. Her only purpose in this is to bring us the recognition of God's good will, working with us and for us for good. This may also bring us to awareness of our own resistance. Indeed, it probably will, but not because she is trying to catch us in a fault. The Spirit comes not to condemn, but to save.

11

Yet if she has to get rough with us to rescue us, she will. The Spirit doesn't always play nice.

I think this is a difficult notion for Anglicans. Every community in every age has its own preferred images of God, shaped more or less to its satisfaction: an angry God or a loving God, a separate god for every purpose (like the ancient Romans) or a single God to preside over everything, a God of the lawyers, a God of the mystics, a God of the theologians, a God of the wayside shrines.

We Anglicans, I think, have at least a secret hankering after a God who is polite, respectful, reasonable—as we, too, would wish to be. And I do not suggest that this picture of God is wrong. It's at least as right as any of the others. But human beings never succeed in grasping God *whole,* in capturing the whole reality. At best, we manage to come up with a few poorly-focused snapshots out of what is more like a motion picture.

There are times, then, when our images of God have to be broken in order to save us from grave misunderstanding. And it is the Spirit, above all, who picks up the wrecker's bar at such times and has at the work of destruction, delivering us from ourselves but also throwing us into a time of uncertainty and anxiety in the process.

We should not be surprised, really. It is all clear from the first moment the Spirit appears in scripture (Gen. 1:2). We used to translate that verse politely as "the Spirit of God moved upon the face of the waters" (Authorized Version). More recently, scholars have suggested that the Hebrew has more force to it and that "Spirit of God" was an idiom for "really big wind." The New Revised Standard Version offers this possible translation: "a mighty wind swept over the face of the waters."

We could put it in a more contemporary vernacular: "the Mother of all storms stirred up the surface of the deep." The Spirit is the Mother of all storms. This is not an easy or friendly or polite image. Many Americans will think of Hurricane Katrina, from which New Orleans has yet to recover fully, or of the series of fierce tornados that struck parts of the United States in 2011. Australians, like Californians, may think of the terrible fire storms that can devastate our landscapes. In an age of increasingly unpredictable climate, every spot in the world must have its tales of the unexpected and daunting. No, it is not an easy or friendly image. And we may be hard pressed to connect the image of storm with the Spirit who also brings us the good news of God's unfailing love.

But we should not be surprised that God can be dangerous and disruptive. Didn't Jesus say, "I came to bring fire to the earth, and how I wish it were already kindled!...Do you think that I have come to bring peace to the earth? No, I tell you, but rather division!" (Luke 12:49, 51). God is known to take the world we are comfortable with and pull it apart and then put it back together in some new way. Which of us has not experienced some of this at one time or another in our lives?

I admit that I occasionally look back with a certain fondness on the quieter days—now so long ago, it seems—when Anglicans had the leisure to debate fine points of "churchmanship" (as we then called it) and nobody was trying to drive anybody else out of the fold. Now, that is impossible. And it is not altogether a loss. The Spirit saw what we were up to, saw that the image of the polite God had too strong a grip on us. The Spirit has put an end to that.

I do not mean to say that the Spirit is directly and personally ripping the church apart. I do not believe that at all. But the Spirit knows our failings: our self-absorption, our petty self-confidence, our lack of real trust in God, our bigotries, our idolatries. If the Spirit wants a wrecking bar, she knows where to find one and when to apply its leverage. And we are, right now, in a world-shaking moment.

The Spirit as builder

But the Spirit does not stop with destruction. The Spirit is a shape-shifter. She dons another of her guises, throws down the wrecking bar, and looks around for hammers and saws. If she can find instruments of destruction in our cowardice and our rigidities, she can find building tools in even the least shred of faith and hope that she finds lurking in us.

The Spirit is looking around for people to build anew, to build better, we hope, to build with open doors and a vast welcome. To raise up shelters where lives can flourish—the lives of individuals and the lives of communities.

The Spirit wants new construction, renewed communities. The Spirit wants us to cross the seemingly eternal divides between rich and poor, between different ethnicities, between men and women, between gay and straight, between evangelical and liberal and catholic, between those who are already believers and those who think they would never care to be one of us.

And when it comes to construction, the Spirit does not necessarily play any nicer than before. In fact, she has no qualms at all about sending raw recruits out to do the dirty work. So no matter how sure you are that you have nothing to offer to this task, do not imagine that you're safe. You remember the Pentecost story. The Spirit descended upon the disciples. She made them behave strangely. She outed them in a hostile environment. She forced them into action.

And that's not all. The Spirit was also in the crowd, even if they did not know it. The Spirit was there opening their ears, enabling them to hear something new, to recognize that it might be important to them, to recognize it as good news.

At the end of Matthew's Gospel, Jesus says to the Eleven that they are to go out and make disciples of the outsiders and baptize them in the name of the Father and of the Son and of the Holy Spirit. We are in much the same spot. Like the disciples, we are basically raw recruits with minimal training. We have had the name of the Spirit invoked over us. And now she is claiming us as her companions in the work.

The best thing, under the circumstances, is to say "yes." Since she does not play nice, she probably will not take "no" for an answer. Recognizing this, of course, will not temper the wind to the shorn lamb, but it will give purpose to the whirlwind we find ourselves in and even some sense of direction and hope as we learn to negotiate it together.

None of us is free just to sit back and wait for someone else to resolve the problems. It is a work for us all. Not that any one of us has to do everything. In fact, no one person can. But the Spirit works by supplying a variety of gifts to the community through a variety of people. What lies ahead for us is a time when we all have something to contribute and every contribution is needed.

When I am tempted to look back nostalgically on the more peaceful days of forty years ago, I also remember that it was actually a boring time. Worse than that, we, as church, thought our only purpose was to keep turning the crank on an eternal ecclesiastical machine. There was no collective sense of new possibility, of unexpected joy, of being showered with grace. At our worst, we did not even think we needed more gifts from the Spirit. We had them all already.

We are blessed to be delivered from those times, even if our present time is threatening and uncertain. The Spirit is at work. The Mother of all storms has been clearing the building site. Now join her in building. Do not wait for someone to hand you a tool kit. You already have one. The Spirit has equipped every one of us with gifts and graces to share with the church at large. Remember Paul's teaching about the gifts of the Spirit:

> Now there are varieties of gifts, but the same Spirit; and there are varieties of services, but the same Lord; and there are varieties of activities, but it is the same God who activates all of them in everyone. To each is given the manifestation of the Spirit for the common good. To one is given through the Spirit the utterance of wisdom, and to another the utterance of knowledge according to the same Spirit, to another faith by the same Spirit, to another gifts of healing by the one Spirit, to another the working of miracles, to another prophecy, to another the discernment of spirits, to another various kinds of tongues, to another the interpretation of tongues. All these are activated by one and the same Spirit, who allots to each one individually just as the Spirit chooses. (1 Cor. 12:4–11)

The inevitable corollary of this is that the Spirit does not give gifts so that we can flaunt them or use them to build up our reputation or magnify ourselves. The Spirit gives us our gifts so that we can share them with everybody else.

Indeed, Paul goes on to say that these gifts find their true significance only insofar as they serve love.

> Love is patient; love is kind; love is not envious or
> boastful or arrogant or rude....Love never ends. But
> as for prophecies, they will come to an end; as for
> tongues, they will cease; as for knowledge, it will come
> to an end....When the complete comes, the partial
> will come to an end....And now faith, hope, and love
> abide, these three; and the greatest of these is love. (1
> Cor. 13:4–5, 8, 10, 13)

Wonderful as our faith is, it will be of no further value when
we stand in the very presence of God. Necessary as hope is
in a world where we need every source of courage we can
find, it is of no further application in the age to come. But
there is no replacement for love. Love is the essence of the
life of the age to come. And it is the element in our life here
and now that already brings us most certainly into the presence of that new and blessed age. The sharing of the gifts of
the Spirit, in love, is our highest calling as faithful, Anglican,
Christian people.

The Spirit, then, is getting ready to do some building. She
has already started handing out tools: tools of knowledge and
wisdom, of prophecy and discernment, of prayer and healing,
of faith and hope, and, above all, of love. Look around you.
Discover your tools. Learn to use them well. And give thanks
that you are living just exactly now, when the Spirit is not
even pretending to play nice because she cares for nothing
but the building of new life and hope.

Of course, the next question is "How do we do that?"
And the answer, in its concrete fullness, is one that we shall
have to find in the *context* where the Spirit summons us to
work and in the very *doing* of the work. For better or worse,
we are not being given full architectural drawings in advance.
But the Spirit is not starting from scratch. She has been, from
the first, the Spirit of creation. She is, equally, the Spirit of
Jesus. We already have from her a broad sense of what is central, which the following chapters will work at identifying.
We also have a sense of what human life, human community,
can be at its fullest and truest. It is embodied in the image of
the age to come that appears in various guises here and there
throughout scripture. It is an age transformed by God's gen-

erosity, an age of *people* transformed by God's generosity. It is a society where we have no need to cover ourselves with false perfections, clothe ourselves in authority, punish ourselves or one another. In that age, God greets the wounded and binds up their traumas and invites us to join in the healing of one another. Isaiah described it as a great feast for all nations on God's mountain (25:6–9). The only people who will be excluded are those who exclude themselves because they cannot bear to see others rejoicing in God's favor.

To put it another way, it is the kind of community that Christina Rossetti was leading us to contemplate in the prayer with which this chapter began:

> O God, only Good, think upon Thy congregation whom Thou hast purchased and redeemed of old. Rule all hearts by Thy Most Holy Spirit; that humbly we may worship Thee, and truthfully confess Thee, owning ourselves unprofitable servants, and in honour preferring one another. To the praise of our Lord Jesus Christ. Amen.

A life of worship, integrity, honesty, humility, and love. This image is not completely new to any of us. We have, in fact, experienced it in our lives, however much we fall short of its perfection. We have experienced it in the church, whatever shortcomings we have found along with it. We look for God's "Most Holy Spirit" to rule our human hearts in ways that will bring us all to a fuller comprehension of it and make it newly available in the life of this age.

2

REFOCUSING ON JESUS

The Spirit does not act as an independent force. We know her as the gift of Jesus, and she directs us back to Jesus at every turn, even if sometimes in unexpected ways or with unexpected results. The building project on which we are launched is not one of those modern commercial developments that begin by clearing the space of every recognizable connection with its past, reducing it to a blank, flat nowhere-in-particular. It begins rather with the clearing of debris, of rubbish, of weeds and brush to reveal the true shape of the terrain. The figure of Jesus marks, and will always mark, the center of the building site.

In Jesus, God has become one of us, so that God knows us now from the inside. And, through Jesus, we at least begin to know God from the inside, too. This is a human kind of knowing; it will not give us a perfect grasp of divine reality. God is, in the technical language of theology, "incomprehensible," even when incarnate in a human being. For that matter, we human beings are not exactly transparent ourselves. No one has an exhaustive knowledge either of oneself or of another person—even the people we know best. Yet, our imperfect knowledge, if animated by love, can still be *real* knowledge of one another. And in Jesus we meet God person to person.

The incarnation, of course, is a paradox. Christians do not believe the incarnation is true because it is easy or obvious. We are, rather, *caught* by it; outrageous as it is, the incarnation of Jesus turns out to be revelatory. The mortal Mary carries in her womb the one who has no beginning, no mother. To see God is death (Exod. 33:20), and yet she will

bring the incomprehensible one to birth and suckle the child
and cradle him in her arms and exchange loving looks with
him. The incarnate Word, immortal origin of life, allows his
human creatures to kill him on a cross, and the impossibility
of God's death destroys not God, but death itself. The crucified one is raised and remains the crucified one, the marks
still in his hands, even as he reveals in himself a new life for
all humankind.

Whatever the Spirit builds will still center on Jesus, the
touchstone by which we gauge every value and the lens
through whom we perceive and understand God, the world,
and our own lives. And so I turn here to another prayer of
Christina Rossetti, an unusual one in that it is addressed directly to Jesus rather than to the first person of the Trinity. It
captures with great economy the relationship between Jesus
and the faithful Christian:

> Lord Jesus, Whom holy Peter loved and Who didst
> much more love Peter, grant us faith all-venturesome
> for Thy sake, hope for an anchor sure and steadfast,
> love responsive to Thy loving call.[7]

Rossetti seems to be thinking here of the narrative in John
21, where Jesus confronts Peter with his betrayal at the time
of Jesus' arrest and death—confronts Peter in order to recall
him into Jesus' full embrace. He confronts him in order to
give him a new beginning. Just so, Christian faith always returns to Jesus for renewal of our relationship with God.

It is a relationship of love, grounded in the eternal and unfailing love of God, not in our own more tentative giving of
self. And it supplies us with a new courage and daring (Rossetti's "faith all-venturesome"), with hope to begin again, and
above all with love, the generosity to share with one another
and the larger world some of the generosity God has shared
with us.

The many images of Jesus

And yet, Jesus is never a simple, fixed figure. Set aside for the
moment that he is God and therefore incomprehensible. It is
enough that he is truly human and therefore can never be

summed up in one or two phrases, one or two images. As with every human being, there is too much depth and complexity for that. From the very beginning Christians have been trying different ways to explain what it is about Jesus that is so immensely important. Even in the three synoptic gospels (Matthew, Mark, and Luke), which are perhaps our simplest and most direct accounts of Jesus, there is significant variation. Matthew's Jesus can sound like the rabbis; Luke's is the best teller of parables; Mark's Jesus ... well, I have had some interesting experience there.

Over my years of teaching New Testament, I would periodically teach an advanced course in the Gospel of Mark. At the beginning of the course, I asked students to read Mark right through several times to help them get Mark's Gospel disentangled in their minds from Matthew and Luke. As we got a few weeks into this process and they had come to know the text better, some students would inevitably say, "You know, I thought I liked Mark's Jesus until I really started reading Mark." I understood their problem.

Mark's Jesus can be abrupt and rude; when the Syrophoenician woman asks him to cast a demon out of her daughter, he dismisses her people as "dogs" (7:27). He gets angry; he chases off the leper he has healed (1:43, harsher in Greek than in English), and responds quite roughly to the father seeking his help for an epileptic boy (9:14–29). He can be kind at times, but he is not particularly gentle. He is, rather, a riveting figure who elicits strong responses, positive and negative, from other characters within the narrative and from Mark's readers.

And the first three gospels are just a beginning. Within the pages of the New Testament, Jesus is portrayed as a rich, complex, and paradoxical figure. He is, among other things, teacher, healer, messiah, lawgiver, priest, prophet, incarnate Word, son of David, sacrificial lamb, suffering servant, savior, pioneer of faith, crucified One, risen One, returning king, judge, punisher of wrong-doing. And this only scrapes the surface. In one way, this multiplicity of images is barely enough to capture what Jesus means for us; but in another way, it is too much. We cannot do justice to all these elements at once, and indeed Christians have never really tried.

All these images remain available in every era. After all, they are right there in the pages of scripture, waiting to be waked up—or to wake us up. But every age makes its choices among them. I was in my forties before this really came home to me—and in a completely unexpected way. I was making my first trip to Italy and decided to limit my stay to just two places I particularly wanted to see. I made that decision because, even though I know a little Italian, I am far from fluent. Most of the time I function with that beautiful language by looking at a text, figuring out what it would be if I turned it back into Latin, and proceeding from there. It's not the ideal skill level for traveling on one's own. Hence my decision to limit my trip to two cities.

First I went to Ravenna to see its ancient churches. The city's heyday was fifteen hundred years ago, in the fifth and sixth centuries, when it was the capital of the Byzantine province of Italy. And many of the churches still have ancient mosaics that show the extraordinary mastery of the Byzantine artists. Mosaics cannot really be caught in photographs because of the way the light shifts as you move around in front of them. I wanted to see them for myself.

They were more wonderful than I had imagined. I will always remember walking into the Church of Sant'Apollinare in Classe (St. Apollinaris at the Naval Base, as it were). The far end of the church is completely clothed in mosaics. In the vault of the apse is a jeweled cross against a night sky filled with stars, the face of Jesus smiling at its center. Below it, on the curved wall of the apse, stands St. Apollinaris in a broad meadow, with scattered trees, flowers, rocks, birds, rabbits. His hands are raised. It could be in prayer. It could be to direct your attention to the cross and the face of Jesus in the sky above him. It could be in welcome. Certainly, he is looking directly out at you as you enter, focusing on *you*, the visitor, with the kindest and most generous of expressions. He is welcoming you into the presence of God, into the parklands of heaven. And you cannot imagine anywhere you would rather be.

There are other extraordinary works of art in Ravenna dating from that relatively short period of time. And the image of Christ and Christianity that they present is remark-

21

ably consistent. Despite the fact that it was a period of warfare and, for the most part, imperial decline—an insecure time—the Christian story communicated there is one of joy and hope and trust in a God who loves us and welcomes us. Even when Jesus is portrayed in imperial robes, as in the apse of San Vitale, he never seems forbidding or remote.

After a few days in Ravenna, I went to Florence. Florence, of course, has flourished over a much longer span of time, from the thirteenth century to the present, so it has not been shaped by a single era in art or culture or religion. But after being in Ravenna, I was struck by one unmistakable difference. Whether I was looking at works of the late Middle Ages or those of the High Renaissance, the art of the Christian faith was heavily weighted toward a very different view of Jesus and his message. The crucifixion was never portrayed directly in Ravenna, but here in Florence, the graphic depiction of Jesus' sufferings, along with the sufferings of the saints, dominated the churches. Another favorite image was that of judgment and the division of the righteous from the unrighteous.

This is not to say that there was nothing welcoming in the art, though such impressions were largely limited to images of the Mother and Child. The adult Jesus is either suffering dreadful pain or glowering at you in judgment. I do not pretend to know the whole explanation for this sea change in Christian imagery. Some of it, I imagine, was the experience of the Black Death in the mid-fourteenth century, which depopulated a Europe already weakened by a prolonged period of cold called "The Little Ice Age" and by the resulting famines. As often with such disasters, there was a search for scapegoats; the persecution of Jews and heretics intensified. No doubt the experience of such widespread suffering and the desire for judgment became intertwined with the Christian faith of those who endured such upheavals.

But whatever the explanation, in Florence I had entered, through the arts, a vastly different understanding of Christian faith. In contrast to the sunny fields of heaven into which Jesus and St. Apollinaris had invited me in Ravenna, I was in the valley of the shadow of death. And if God still seemed to be watching over me, it was more to make sure that I did not commit any heresy or succumb to temptation than to offer the comfort of the good shepherd's rod and staff.

At the time, I did not understand how deeply all this was affecting me. I was feeling rather low, maybe a bit homesick. I did find one notable exception to the prevailing grimness in the works of Fra Angelico at the Museo di San Marco, but on the whole, I found myself gravitating to the more pagan side of the Renaissance, which seemed friendlier: think of Botticelli's *Birth of Venus* or *Primavera*. I went off, at a friend's suggestion, to the Museum of Modern Art. (Yes, there is one in Florence, "modern" meaning mostly nineteenth century.) There I found welcoming, sunny landscapes, some of them by a favorite American painter, John Singer Sargent, which cheered me up for a time. But I came to understand later that what I was going through was a kind of deep spiritual deprivation.

Again on a friend's recommendation, I took a day trip to the city of Lucca. It was a thriving place in the twelfth century, so its oldest churches are Romanesque, not the later Gothic. And in the cathedral, there is a famous image called the *Volto Santo,* the Holy Face. It is actually a life-sized sculpture of Christ clothed in a long robe, with arms outstretched as if on the cross. The exact origins of the image are obscure, but it has Byzantine connections. And when I saw it I was suddenly transported back to Ravenna: this was once again the welcoming Jesus I had seen there. And I found to my surprise that my eyes were tearing up. I was experiencing something much more than just aesthetic pleasure. I was meeting once again a Jesus who offers hope and not simply judgment, a Jesus I had not seen much of for the previous week. I was glad that I was standing in a church, where wet cheeks were not likely to draw the kind of odd looks they might in a museum.

This is not to say that the images of Jesus I found in Florence were wrong. They, too, were rooted in scripture. My point, rather, is that different circumstances call different aspects of Jesus to the fore, and it is possible for the image that is central in one age to become unhelpful or even oppressive in another. The images of Jesus I found at Florence, like those at Ravenna, have sustained faithful people through good and bad times. They also have their dangers.

The serenity of heaven shares space in the Ravenna mosaics with the glittering image of the imperial court of Justinian and Theodora—a court distinguished for piety and the arts, but also for treachery and violence, and for its failure to deal constructively with a schism that still afflicts Christianity, the break between Chalcedonian and non-Chalcedonian believers. The serenity of Ravenna's Jesus may have covered a multitude of imperial sins or even made the empire look like a this-worldly counterpart of the age to come.

In Florence, the image of the suffering Jesus offered great encouragement to a suffering people by assuring them that God had already lived their human distress with them. Yet, I could not help but connect it with a certain callousness in the religion of the time that could justify terrible levels of suffering among the poor and marginal as something divinely willed, or could even inflict such suffering on others through institutions like the Inquisition—and do it in the very name of the suffering God. There have been dreadful moments when Christian spirituality seems to have made a pact with sadism.

The accompanying focus on Jesus as final judge, while it could give hope to those suffering injustice, was rife with opportunities for corruption. How often, when Christians invoke images of the Last Judgment, do we imagine ourselves as the accused? In our apocalyptic fantasies, it is always the *others* whom we hand over confidently to destruction.

The point here is not to say that these images are intrinsically wrong, but to acknowledge our human propensity to turn what is good to evil purposes, in order to reinforce our own sense of being God's chosen and consign the rest of humanity to eternal disfavor. Particularly at times of great change, we have to become conscious of this and think carefully about how we shall speak and think of Jesus in the future. What images will move to the fore?

This is a matter of refocusing, not of changing the Jesus in whom we repose our faith. It is a matter of recognizing that there are many aspects to Jesus, including some that may have sunk into the background and others whose misuse has made their capacity to communicate good news problematic. The crucifixion, for example, was seldom portrayed in ancient Christian art. Then it came to the fore to speak to the famines and plagues of the late Middle Ages. It does not follow that it will always retain the centrality it acquired then. Indeed, for many Christians it has already passed out of common use.

No single image of Jesus dominates Christianity today. Different traditions tend to follow different leads. Apocalyptic Christianity portrays Jesus as the severe judge of outsiders, but the gracious rescuer of insiders. Evangelicals focus on Jesus as the willing sacrifice who makes forgiveness possible. Liberal Protestants tend to see him as an ethical teacher or as the prophetic figure who practiced justice and maintained integrity even in the face of condemnation and death. In Anglican stained glass, he is the Good Shepherd, rescuing lost sheep. He is the comforter of the sorrowful. He welcomes children. He is the holy figure who breaks down barriers by eating with sinners and invites the marginalized to rub elbows with the privileged.

All these images have roots in scripture. Each apparently has something to say to people today. But none of them is *the* Jesus of the New Testament or *the* Jesus for all time. The Jesus we first come to know is just a starting point in our life's growing intimacy with God. Our knowledge of any person is constantly changing. It may grow or shrink, depending on circumstances and the character of the relationship. No one is fully known at first meeting. Knowing a person is not like knowing *about* someone. To know a person is to be in a living relationship with that person. We come to know God as one who interacts with us person to person. We must expect faithful knowledge to grow and deepen and, yes, find its focus changing at times.

Jesus the priest

How Jesus will prove most intelligible to people in our own time will become clear only through a process of ongoing discernment by the whole Christian community. I am going to suggest two images that I think speak to the world in which

I live, knowing they are by no means the only possibilities. My hope is not to settle the matter, but to stimulate ongoing reflection on how we see Jesus becoming significant in the world where we live. This reflection is part of the work of construction that we are undertaking with the Spirit's help and guidance.

The first image I take up here is that of *priest*. I use it, however, in a way somewhat different from the image that may first spring to mind, which is a priesthood particularly associated with a sacrificial cult or practice of religion. The problem with this association is that sacrifice, in the sense of the offering of animals or other food on a blazing altar, is no longer a living practice for most Western people. There is always a danger in unanchored metaphors or images: it is too easy to attribute false or unreal meanings to practices no longer alive among us.

In Hebrew tradition, however, priesthood has always had a broader role, of which animal sacrifice was only an incidental part. The old priest Eli, under whom the young Samuel served, remained a priest in terms of his intimacy with God long after he handed over the heavy labor of sacrifice over to his sons. He lived, quite literally, in God's house, the temple at Shiloh. And when Samuel first heard the voice of God but did not recognize who spoke, it was Eli who could tell him who it was and how to respond (1 Samuel 1–2).

In the most basic sense, a priest is one who lives in the presence of God and can assist others who enter that presence. A priest is anyone who can help you stand in the presence of God and understand something about what you experience there. This kind of priesthood is still very much alive. In fact, it is going on all around us, all through our lives. We all perform priestly acts, and we are all ministered to in priestly ways—not only by ordained priests, but by old friends, by wise mentors, even by complete strangers.[8]

Such priesthood is not limited to a narrowly religious context. God, after all, is not constrained by the boundaries of religion; God is at work everywhere, at all times. "The Edge," a poem by the Australian poet Rosemary Dobson, offers a compelling account of priesthood, not least because she does

not try to pin it down. The poem does not "explain" things.
It lives in the mystery.

> Three times to the world's end I went,
> Three times returned as one who brings
> Tidings of light beyond the dark
> But voiceless stays, still marvelling.
>
> After great pain I had great joy
> Three times that never else I knew;
> The last reflection of its light
> Fades from the pupils of my eyes.
>
> Webbed by the world again I walk
> The mazy paths that women tread
> Watchful lest any harm should come
> To those who journeyed back with me.
>
> But still, as Lazarus who was born
> Again beyond the edge of death,
> I see the world half otherwise
> And tremble at its mysteries.[9]

The poet uses some religious language here, but the poem
could be related to any number of different human experiences. And so it is with our lives: our encounters with the
Holy are often difficult to express or to explain, and we are
profoundly relieved to find someone who can speak to some
part of it or even sit quietly with us. The person in whose face
we see a light of understanding, but who has no need to take
charge of our experience or make it conform to his or her expectations—this is our priest.

Such priesthood is by no means limited to the ordained.
They are important rather as a sacrament of it. It may have
been Archbishop William Temple who once said, with reference to the Eucharist, that the bread on the altar could not
be holy if all bread were not holy, and we could not know
that all bread is holy without seeing that the bread on the
altar is holy. The bread of the Eucharist does not monopolize
holiness; it calls our attention to itself so that it can send our
attention back out to the bread of the world, which is holy
because it maintains life. This is the bread we pray for day

by day, the bread that all humanity needs. God makes the bread of the altar the Body of Christ so that we can live as the body of Christ in the world and share our bread with others. In the same way, ordained priests serve as sacraments of the priesthood we all share—this priesthood that helps people find themselves in God's presence and then helps them understand who this God is.

There is a tremendous thirst for the Holy in our world. People spend time and money hoping to encounter it. Admittedly, they sometimes look in very odd places, but that is nothing new. And there is a certain "fast food" mentality about much of it. "I'd like my order of the Holy with a Palestrina motet and a dollop of Buddhist heavy metal—and a side order of a really beautiful sunset." I don't mean simply to mock such eclectic religious searching, for it can lead to a significant encounter with God. But there is a certain narcissism in this mixing of traditions, an assumption that I can tailor my encounter with God to my particular tastes without having to be challenged by it. It is a consumerist approach, and such an approach, being focused on my personal satisfaction, can in fact get in the way of true encounter with the Holy. The hunger for "fast food" spiritual experience is being ministered to by quite an array of gurus, seers, television preachers, dubious healers, and drumming retreat leaders. Most of these, I fear, offer an impoverished diet in comparison to what any of the world religions with their depth of spiritual tradition can offer. In my experience Anglicans offer a kind of "slow food" spirituality. We figure it will be worth the wait, and the wait might even do us good.

No matter what sort of spiritual diet we find most appealing, the point remains. The Holy is real. Plenty of people who do not go to church know full well that they have in fact been in the presence of the Holy, whether they call it "God" or not. They have encountered it in the forests and mountains and oceans, in music and poetry, in the communion of friends, in the making of love, in the creating of art or in its presence, even in times of distress and illness and sorrow. In many ways, our lives bring us up against this something *more*—more than the surface of things, more than the merely observable, a sense of having been in the presence of ultimate reality. Plenty of us who go to church have had these experiences too, and in the same diversity of contexts. God is not confined to what goes on in the sanctuary. But what goes on in the sanctuary is important to us because it helps us understand our varied experiences of the Holy and brings it into conversation with the more mundane parts of life, so we can discover how to live in ways that are responsive to our encounter with God.

We need one another for this. This is the importance of priesthood. You can encounter God without anybody else's help. God knows how to make that happen. But learning to understand our experience and to grow in it takes help. This is what our priests give us, and this is what we, in our priestly moments, give to others.

When I speak of Jesus as priest, then, it is this aspect of priesthood I have in mind. We see Jesus in this role throughout the gospel narratives as he teaches and heals. We can see people's relationships with God being transformed in his presence. Take, for example, the woman with the hemorrhage (Mark 5:25–34). She was not only ill; she was rendered unclean by her illness. She had no business being out in a crowd where her mere touch could render the people around her unclean and therefore render their devotions unclean and presumably unacceptable to God without their ever knowing it. Simply hearing the stories of what Jesus did and taught had emboldened her to seek healing from him. She hoped to do it secretly, since she still did not quite trust God to have any care for an unclean person. But when Jesus turned around and singled her out, she could no longer avoid recognizing the love of God. This was not simply a physical healing, but a profound encounter with God, its meaning made clear to her by Jesus' priestly ministry.

The principal scriptural source for speaking of Jesus as priest is the Epistle to the Hebrews, a mysterious book whose author, as the early Christian theologian Origen said, is known to God alone. Here, Jesus is interpreted as "a high priest forever according to the order of Melchizedek" (6:20). At the same time, Hebrews acknowledges the basic literal truth that Jesus was a layman. He was not a priest in terms of Israelite religion, because he was not descended from the tribe of Levi and the family of Aaron (7:13–14). He was not an ordained rabbi, either, as he had had no teacher to instruct him and ordain him. Jesus was a layman.

This may be one reason why the author of Hebrews chose the analogy of Melchizedek to interpret Jesus' priesthood. Melchizedek was not a descendant of Aaron. In fact, he was not even an Israelite. He was a Gentile. He stood outside the whole religious system of ordination. His priestly act was to bring Abraham bread and wine and to pronounce a blessing over him as Abraham returned from defeating the marauding kings of the East. And Abraham acknowledged him as a true priest who could assist him as he stood in the presence of God (Gen. 14:18–20).

From Jesus this priesthood devolves upon the whole Christian people. In 1 Peter, we hear ourselves addressed as "a chosen race, a royal priesthood, a holy nation" (2:9). Every one of us has some experience of being in God's presence—an experience and understanding that is crucial for the world around us, even if we do not know exactly when or for whom. Even for the ordained, this priesthood—the one they already had before they were ordained and still have— is basic. Ordained priesthood can become a starved shadow unless it is enmeshed with the priestly life more broadly conceived.

Jesus' priesthood emerges from his identity as a person completely at home with God, completely intimate with God. People could see this intimacy in his words and actions, from the very beginning of his preaching. Mark's account of the initiation of his ministry is brief but astonishing: "After John was arrested, Jesus came to Galilee, proclaiming the good news of God, and saying, 'The time is fulfilled, and the kingdom of God has come near; repent, and believe in the good news'" (Mark 1:14–15). Typically, we hear the words "the kingdom of God has come near" as a threat. Only a priest with intimate knowledge of God would dare reverse that and declare that God's nearness is good news, not bad. Our English translations have gone back to making it sound like bad news when they tell us that the correct response is "repentance." Doesn't that mean that we are in deep trouble and we had better show remorse or we are done for? No, as

William Temple pointed out a long time ago, we ought to translate the Greek word *metanoeite* not as "repent," but as "get a new mind."[10] Throw out your old assumptions. God is not coming to punish but to seek and save the lost, including you.

Jesus, as priest, identifies with us, stands at our side. This is where a priest is supposed to stand. As Hebrews says, a priest is one who can "sympathize with our weaknesses" (4:15). But, at the same time, the priest has to know God and be willing to speak the truth about God. It is odd that the truth about God that we are least willing to hear is that God is love—worse yet, that God is in love with you. "The kingdom of God has come near; change your mind, get a new mind, and believe the good news."

Jesus did not understand this as a kind of happy-go-lucky, escapist message. He repeatedly predicted his own betrayal and crucifixion. He knew how this world is filled with fear and hatred. He knew the cost of being God's priest in this world. And he was willing, if necessary, to pay it. For him, the cost of priesthood was the giving of his life, first by pouring it out as teacher and healer, then by sacrificing it on the cross both to expose the evils of the world and to show the steadfastness of God's love. This sacrifice was not an act of obedience to law, but the ultimate proclamation of God's drawing near to us in love.

Jesus the priest is well represented in a painting by Henry Ossawa Tanner, an African-American artist working at the turn of the last century. *Nicodemus Visiting Jesus* draws its subject matter from John 3. The two men sit, not quite facing each other, on a flat rooftop of the sort the artist saw in the Holy Land, near an open stairwell. It is dusk, and lamplight shines up the stairs from a room below, illuminating the scene in a sidelong way that evokes for me Henry Vaughan's poem about Nicodemus' visit:

> There is in God (some say)
> A deep, but dazzling darkness; as men here
> Say it is late and dusky, because they
>   See not all clear. . . . [11]

The intensity of the two figures, looking directly at one another, tells us that their conversation is reaching into great depths. According to John's Gospel, Nicodemus understood little of it. Yet, he understood that Jesus had entered God's presence and was at home there in a way that Nicodemus could barely imagine. John's Gospel says that Jesus actually incarnates that presence; and Tanner hints at this by a faint glow that rests on Jesus' head covering and a finger he has raised that gestures upward and yet also points slightly toward himself. Yet, the emphasis here is not on Jesus' divinity, but on his ability to accompany another into the presence of God—on his priesthood.[12]

Jesus continues to be priest. Jesus can still reconnect us with God, can still stand alongside us with perfect understanding when we encounter God, wherever that may be. Jesus invites us into God's own intimate family, God's circle of friends, the circle of Jesus' sisters and brothers. He lived out his earthly priesthood right in the thick of ordinary people like us. Forget that some of his followers *eventually* became saints and extraordinary priests in their own right; in the gospels we see them stumbling, falling over themselves, getting it all wrong, just like us.

Their growth into something more was not a condition of their encounter with God, but a result. Only in the presence of God do we begin to perceive the kind of humanity that we shall grow into by God's grace. As another New Testament writer says: "Beloved, we are God's children now; what we will be has not yet been revealed. What we do know is this: when he is revealed, we will be like him, for we will see him as he is" (1 John 3:2).

This image of Jesus as priest, I suspect, is as important now as it has ever been. In a world that continues to be hungry for God—despite all the repeated predictions that religion is going to fade away any minute now—Jesus the priest, who offers to stand by us in God's presence, is still relevant.

Jesus as lover

The second image I want to explore is that of Jesus the bridegroom, or, more broadly, the lover. This language may be unfamiliar to Christians today. Jesus refers to himself as "the bridegroom" once in explaining why his disciples did not fast (Mark 2:18–20; Matt. 9:14–17; Luke 5:33–39). And in John's Gospel, John the Baptist uses the same image for Jesus (3:29). This may seem like a slender foundation to build on. But behind it, of course, lies a biblical text that was vastly influential throughout most of Jewish and Christian history, even though we have largely ignored it for the last hundred years or so—"The Song of Songs, which is Solomon's" (to give it its full title). On the surface, it is simply a book of love songs, quite racy love songs, at that, as you can see if you read recent translations such as that of Marcia Falk[13] or the one by Ariel Bloch and Chana Bloch.[14] But the faithful have been reading the Song of Songs as a love story between God and Israel, between God and the church, between God and the individual soul since at least the second century. A vast array of commentary has grown up around this one little book for this exact reason.

The Song of Songs uses the language of erotic attraction to tell this story. But if you prefer, the language of friendship can serve the same purpose. Jesus, in John's Gospel, talks about the love between him and his disciples, one of whom is even called "the beloved disciple." He calls them his friends and says to them, "No one has greater love than this, to lay down one's life for one's friends" (John 15:13). He invites their love in return.

We sometimes distinguish love pretty sharply from friendship. Yes, erotic attraction and friendship are not exactly the same thing, but they are related to each other. Let me explain how I'm using the word "friend" here. I do not mean "acquaintance." I do not mean "business associate." I do not mean the people on your Facebook page. I do not mean just anybody whose company you might be able to endure for an evening if you had to. True friends are people for whom we feel desire, even if it is not sexual desire. We *want* to be with them. We feel more truly ourselves in their company. This quality of desire and fulfillment is what connects these two kinds of relationship.

The image of Jesus as lover runs deep in Christian tradition. Here are two short examples from seventeenth-century poets. The first is by Henry Vaughan, who wrote during the Puritan regime in England. The Puritans had banned the use of the *Book of Common Prayer* and other elements of Anglican worship, and Vaughan fell back on personal prayer for his primary sense of connection with God. He particularly loved the early morning hours for this purpose, and this little poem starts with a call to prayer in the dawn. The imagery of dawn then gradually gives way to images of the arrival of spring, with Vaughan borrowing imagery from the Song of Songs. ("Turtles" here are an archaism for "turtledoves.") And it ends with a surprise.

> Unfold, unfold! Take in his light
> Who makes thy cares more short than night.
> The joys, which with his Day-star rise,
> He deals to all, but drowsy eyes:
> And what the men of this world miss,
> Some drops and dews of future bliss.
> 　　Hark! how his winds have changed their note,
> And with warm whispers call thee out.
> The frosts are past, the storms are gone:
> And backward life at last comes on.
> The lofty groves in express joys
> Reply unto the turtle's voice,
> And here in dust and dirt, O here
> The lilies of his love appear![15]

The lilies of God's love appear right here in the dust and dirt of ordinary human life. This is a passionate image of both yearning and presence. Whether you think of it in erotic terms or as expressive of other kinds of love makes little difference.

Here's another expression of love—this time in a familial sense—in a poem by Thomas Traherne. Its topic is the Bible, but you may be surprised at what Traherne finds there. Generally when a sentence begins, "The Bible says...," one expects to hear something negative—an attack on someone, a prohibition, an angry denunciation. Traherne had experienced that kind of Bible-reading from the Puritans of his time. But in his own reading, he found something else—something surprising enough to him that the poem starts off with a kind of stutter of disbelief:

That! That! There I was told
That I the son of God was made,
His image. O divine! And that fine gold,
    With all the joys that here do fade,
Are but a toy, compared to the bliss
Which heavenly, God-like, and eternal is.

That we on earth are kings;
    And, tho we're cloth'd with mortal skin,
Are inward cherubins, have angels' wings;
    Affections, thoughts, and minds within,
Can soar through all the coasts of Heaven and earth;
And shall be sated with celestial mirth.[16]

This is a passionate poem, filled with the ecstatic surprise of
someone discovering that he is actually *loved* and claimed as
God's own child.

My lasting visual impression of Jesus the lover has come
from a painting by Giovanni Bellini called *Christ Blessing*.
Jesus looks directly out at us. His right hand is raised in blessing, which means we notice the mark of the nail in his open
palm. His left hand holds a tall staff, identified by its red color
as the staff that carries the banner of the resurrection over-
head, beyond the frame of the picture. The time is early dawn
in the springtime. A bird perches in a still leafless tree; two
rabbits nuzzle each other in the meadow. And in the distance
three women are on the path together. Their physical stance
suggests that they are burdened—perhaps with jars of spices,
probably with grief. They are on their way to the tomb, but
Jesus is already gone from there. And, wonder of wonders,
he is giving us his blessing even before he appears to Mary
Magdalene. His expression is one of complete serenity. The
naked torso emphasizes his human vulnerability, and you can
still trace the wound in his side. But he is fully and beautifully
alive. The rays of light about his head bespeak divinity, but
there is nothing in this beautiful person, just on the verge of
a smile, to fear.[17]

Jesus, you see, is in love with you. If this makes you feel a
little odd, it is not an occasion to worry. Jesus is the most pa-
tient and tactful of lovers. You can have time to get used to
the idea. But don't expect him to give up. He will not rest

content until our lives are transformed and renewed by his love.

This love will not be something purely private, a kind of possession to be hoarded away. The point is for us not only to be loved by Jesus, but to become lovers ourselves. "Love one another as I have loved you" (John 15:12). If this feels beyond us (and it does, much of the time), it's because we have not yet truly comprehended how deeply we are loved. God sees in every one of us a particular beauty that we our- selves may be blind to. God's vision is not impeded by our pretensions, our self-deceptions, our narcissism, our general cluelessness. It penetrates through all that and *still* finds something in us beautiful, desirable. And the strange experi- ence of discovering and accepting God's love leads us to a new understanding that there is also a deeply attractive beauty in our fellow human beings, however well hidden it may be in some cases!

The love of Jesus, then, draws us not just toward Jesus the lover, but into a circle of lovers. By accepting Jesus' love, we find resources of love in ourselves that we did not know we had. We are not limited to being mere consumers of love. We have the capacity to become creators and sharers of it. Love has the extraordinary capacity to make us stronger and freer people than we thought we were. In our world, there has been too much sex disconnected from love and too much "friend- ship" reduced to a kind of business opportunity. This image of Jesus offers a countervailing inspiration, pointing us to- ward a braver and more generous humanity and giving us the resources to grow toward it.[18]

This is not all, of course. I could name other images of Jesus that have been and still are immensely important to my own faith. He is the child of Bethlehem, God surrendering Godself entirely to our human power. With his family, he is the refugee in a foreign land. He is the teller of parables that bring enlightenment. He is the innocent victim who never bends to his persecutors. One image that has been largely neglected all

these centuries, but may yet be important for us today, is the
Jesus of the wild animals. As Mark tells us, Jesus "was with
the wild beasts" after his temptation in the wilderness, "and
the angels waited on him" (1:13). That he found the natural
world a refuge, a place of restoration, a home speaks directly
to us in an age of ecological crisis.[19]

Jesus will never be summed up in a few words or titles or
images. And no one age can do justice to every aspect of who
he is. But in every age we will, of necessity, make some deci-
sions about what images of Jesus are God's particular, gracious gifts for our times and places. In large part, this is a
process of looking within and rediscovering how Jesus has
been addressing *us*. What is it about Jesus that most deeply
moves you? Your answers may be different from the ones I
have suggested here. Good. Take them seriously. Tell the
world about the beauty and grace that you have seen.

The most important test of our images' validity is simply
this: Jesus called his message *euangelion*, "good news." Are
the images of Jesus we offer the world good news? If they are,
they will find a response. And they will produce the consequences that Christina Rossetti asked for in the prayer with
which this chapter began.

Lord Jesus, Whom holy Peter loved and Who didst
much more love Peter, grant us faith all-venturesome
for Thy sake, hope for an anchor sure and steadfast,
love responsive to Thy loving call.

It is the love between Jesus and Peter that makes the rest possible. And it gives rise to courage, to constancy, to generosity.
Good news, indeed!

3

CELEBRATING GIFTS
RECEIVED

> O God of peace, who hast taught us that in returning
> and rest we shall be saved, in quietness and in confi-
> dence shall be our strength: By the might of thy Spirit
> lift us, we pray thee, to thy presence, where we may be
> still and know that thou art God; through Jesus Christ
> our Lord. *Amen.*[20]

"Lift us to thy presence"—this phrase captures an important
part of what religion is about. The presence of God that we
seek is a place of consolation, refreshment, and delight. It is
also a place where we are formed anew and given energy to
live in our daily world in ways that reflect God's love and
generosity. We may have met God at the very margins of life,
but the relationship thus formed turns out to be our center.
As we Christians try to find our way through the uncertainties of the present, we treasure the ways in which we have
been brought into God's presence in the past and we do not
abandon them. But we find here, as with the image of Jesus,
that what is old can and will become new. The graces of the
past are not eternally fixed in their finest details. Indeed,
sometimes they are taken up and reused in new building proj-
ects.

Jesus, of course, has many ways of speaking to the world.
One might ask whether the Anglican tradition in particular
is so important that it really has to go on being a factor in
the Christian community. Is it really vital that it survive? In
the middle of the last century, some Anglicans suggested that

our vocation might be to disappear into the larger ecumenical movement that seemed so full of promise at the time, when in the heady days of Vatican II it seemed as if the churches might really be on the verge of overcoming some age-old divisions. Since then, the old divisions have only widened further, with a few new rifts added for good measure. If Anglican Christianity is to disappear in our day, it seems more likely to happen through fragmentation than through merger, and it is less easy to feel positive about the consequences.

I believe our Anglican identity is worth maintaining—not because I think it is the only way of being Christian, which it clearly is not, but because it offers a particular assemblage of gifts whose loss would make the church (and therefore the world as a whole) poorer. This is not, I think, pure stubbornness on my part, though I do not entirely discount the possibility of that. We do, after all, have a certain element in our tradition that I think of as the *harrumph!* factor. It allows us take refuge in a certain level of bluster when change threatens. A lot of Anglican jokes center around it, exploiting our reluctance to contemplate even the slightest alteration. But what motivates me to hold on to my Anglican identity is rather a sense of gratitude—above all, gratitude for *worship,* which has always been the key Anglican focus. Worship is our most obvious reason for existence. It's what we *do.* And we do it both privately and together—but above all, together: "By the might of thy Spirit lift us, we pray thee, to thy presence...." This lifting up happens over and over again in our common prayer. We are a community of worship.

And something else of great value emerges from this focus on common prayer: a breadth of spirituality. Truly common prayer requires multiple voices. In the Episcopal Church of my teen years, I found that multiplicity reflected in an extraordinary wealth of spiritual lore. Tract racks actually had little collections of extracts from people from earlier centuries, like Brother Lawrence and Lancelot Andrewes. The hymnal was full of wonderful texts from the whole span of Christian history. (And, yes, some not-so-wonderful ones, too.) In the worship of my local Episcopal parish I was given access to a broad historical diversity that made room, here and now, for many different ways of prayer. I was not told to fit myself into a single, prescribed pattern of spirituality; I was given a world in which to grow.

So I feel very strongly that it is not a selfish thing that we want to see this tradition survive and grow. God can and does make Godself known through the Methodist Church and the Roman Catholic Church and the Eastern Orthodox and the Baptists and the whole bright array. God is not limited to a single Christian tradition. To suppose such a thing is to commit idolatry. But for any tradition to hold cheap the particular gifts that it has received would be unfaithful. We should share them. We should remember that there are uncountable numbers of people who might well find themselves as blessed by this tradition as we have been. Many of them have not been born yet. We are bearers and transmitters of these gifts for them. If not us, who?

Sacrament

What, then, is so important in our tradition of worship? Let me draw two elements from it to explore further: the sacraments and the scriptures. The theologically educated reader may think, "Not very distinctive! Every church that came through the Reformation exalts these two elements." Yes. Usually, they name them in the reverse order, as "Word and Sacrament." That ordering is not accidental, nor is my choice of taking up sacraments first. The sacraments have been more closely identified with the catholic strand in Anglicanism and scripture with the evangelical strand, but my personal preference for catholic theology and piety is not the reason for my choice. My reason is rather that all Anglicans have historically been shaped by a book that is particularly concerned not with theology as such but with public worship. It is the way sacrament and scripture are joined in the larger whole of worship that is most characteristic of us Anglicans. Because the sacraments are actions as well as words, they have the power to shape the basic environment of prayer.

To put it in colloquial terms, we worship a broad-spectrum God. God communicates through words—and equally through things. Words are immensely important to us, as to all Reformation churches. But so, too, are the sacraments, which are present in our worship not as intellectual information or theological requirements but as rites. As with the heavens, "There is neither speech nor language; but their voices are heard among them. Their sound is gone out into all lands; and their words into the ends of the world" (Ps. 19:3–4).[21] Sometimes the language of things and gestures is deeper and more powerful than words.

Human beings are not just minds or souls who happen to be stuck in bodies. Our bodies are not mere instruments of the spirit. Human beings *are* bodies as well souls and spirits, bodies given life by the breath of God. All three elements participate in our personhood. It seems like a clumsy way to put a human being together, but nothing less than this captures our human reality. And we cannot imagine that God's mode of communication is less broad, generous, and complex than God's mode of creation. Why would God create something as complex as humanity and then try to communicate with us by words alone?

Another way to think of it is to point out that sacraments are a carrying on of the incarnation. The two go together. In the incarnation, God communicates Godself through the material realities of the world. It's often said that Anglicans are particularly attached to the incarnation. This may be partly a reaction against the Puritans. After all, they abolished the celebration of Christmas while they were in power in England, and we took exception to that—reasonably enough. But, of course, it has much deeper roots—in scripture and in the early Greek theologians. Medieval Western Catholicism pushed the cross into the foreground, as we have seen. Anglicans actually represent a kind of rebalancing by one strand of Western Christianity in the direction of the older Greek theology, summed up in St. Athanasius's famous words: God became a human being so that humanity might become God.

Of course, it is never a simple "either/or." Bethlehem and Calvary need each other. Neither makes full sense without the other. And not even together will they make much sense without the miracle of Easter. How interesting that Western Christians have traditionally called the ancient church in Jerusalem built on the land thought to be the site of the crucifixion and burial of Jesus the Church of the Holy Sepulcher.

41

To the Greeks, it is the *Anastasis*, the Church of the Resurrection. As in the mosaics of Ravenna or Bellini's *Christ Blessing*, the resurrection pronounces benediction on the entire story.

There is no either/or choice, then, between incarnation and cross. But it is still significant where we focus our gaze. Did the Word become incarnate in Jesus just as a necessary preliminary, a kind of qualifying round, to make him eligible to suffer on the cross? Or was the suffering on the cross rather the price God paid in order to become incarnate, to identify as intimately and completely as possible with us? I don't know that all Anglicans would answer this question in the same way—especially when it is put as baldly as this. But our worship, at least, tends toward the second (the cross as the cost God was willing to bear for the sake of the incarnation), though strongly evangelical Anglicans may take exception to this view. And such an emphasis on incarnation connects seamlessly with the sacraments.

The sacraments, to be sure, make use of words, but their power to communicate lies in their use of concrete objects and places: the basin of water for the baptismal washing; the table for our eucharistic feast, set with bread and wine and the vessels that contain them; the laying on of hands in prayer, the joining of hands in an exchange of peace; the signing with the cross in blessing, the anointing with oils for healing and restoration. All tangible things. These are our sacramental center. And spreading out from this center, sacramental Christianity is replete with bodily movement, from kneeling to standing to bowing and on to processions or pilgrimage. We are familiar with objects whose use calls forth reverence, like the image of the cross, or embodies reverence, like candles and incense. We expect worship to appeal sensually to the ear through poetic speech and music, to the eye through image and color, to the taste in bread and wine, to the sense of smell in incense and fragrant oils, to the touch of human hands reaching out in love.

This move toward a certain beauty and richness in worship has been characteristic of Anglicans from our beginnings. Even at a time of deliberate simplification in the late sixteenth and early seventeenth centuries, we produced an explosion of great religious music from such composers as Gibbons and Tomkins. Restraint can be good, to be sure: when St. Paul was trying to damp down the charismatic free-for-all at Corinth, he insisted that worship be conducted "decently and in order" (1 Cor. 14:40). It is a good rule as far as it goes, but it cannot take us very far, for it is essentially negative. It tells us what to avoid rather than what to aim at. Our instinct has been to set our sights higher: to worship "in the beauty of holiness" (Ps. 29:2, 96.9; 1 Chron. 16:29).

We want the worship of the church to be rich in ways appropriate to its setting. For as soon as we speak of "beauty," we know it will not be one rule for all. The liturgical trend in English-speaking cultures of late has tended to follow the modernist aesthetic canon of "less is more." Juan Cabrero Oliver, a Puerto Rican friend who is also a priest and a liturgical scholar, said to me once, "Only a northern European would say, 'Less is more.' For a Latino, more is always more." It is true, in a way, even of Latin American modernism. The arts we employ must make cultural sense—they must have communicative power in the cultural and social context of worship. A single formula will not work equally well everywhere, which is one reason Anglicans have resisted absolute uniformity. And culture does not stand still, which means that the beauty of worship is always in the process of being created anew.

Local realities have always been a factor for us. Our reformers understood that English was not the language for Welsh worship. (To our shame, they failed to apply the same principle to Cornwall and Ireland.) In the eighteenth century, the Scots created their Communion Office and the newly independent Americans their first *Book of Common Prayer.* The Prayer Book itself was being "indigenized" among Anglicans outside the Church of England, and this process of diversification and local inculturation has broadened out over the centuries into many languages and all aspects of liturgy. For worship must speak to the senses as well as the mind and must give us, as worshippers, opportunity to speak with our bodies as well as our souls and spirits.

Our God is a broad-spectrum God. Humanity, created in God's image, is a complex creature. God has determined that the only way to communicate effectively with us is to draw as near to us as possible, indeed, to assume our very life. The sacramental dimension of worship responds to the reality of creation and incarnation by functioning on the broadest "bandwidth" available in any given place and time. We are indeed called to worship not just in decency and order, but in the beauty of holiness.

I cannot imagine what sort of identity Anglicans would want to claim that did not include this incarnational and sacramental element. This is not the sort of thing that can be dismissed as "merely" traditional. Rather, this element is a treasured gift. God has met us here again and again, and we therefore return again and again to where we have known God's presence. The Holy One does not always seem to turn up on call—at least, not in ways that we can appreciate. We are not always shaken, calmed, enlightened, transformed by worship. But there are times when encounter does happen, and, at the very least, we remember each time why we have come. We have come because God really has met us here.

Scripture

The other, equally important element in our worship is the *word*. The Gospel of John says that the Word is God. But beware: this can be misunderstood. The center of our faith is not words, not even divinely inspired words. The Bible is not the heart of Christian faith. Any effort to put it in that position is heretical at best; at worst, it places us in danger of idolatry. The center of our faith is the divine Word of creative power, incarnate not in black marks on paper—or papyrus or parchment—but in flesh.

One could make a case for saying that if Christianity had to survive either on sacraments alone or on scripture alone, it would do better with sacraments. They remind us that faith is not primarily a matter of ideas to consider or beliefs to hold, but a shaping of life, lived out in the light of the good news, in the light of God's own participation in that life, in the light of a hope that dares to keep its head up even in the face of the most terrible circumstances.

Of course, we do not have to make such a choice. Most forms of Christianity agree on the importance of both word and sacrament, however much they vary in the ways they balance them. But for fourteen hundred years, before Gutenberg's invention of printing with moveable type, the church did live primarily from the sacraments, if only because of the rarity of books and of the ability to read them. That period produced some strange distortions of the Christian message, but it also produced plenty of saints and great heights of holiness and intimacy with God in Christ.

But focus now on the scriptures. The word means "writings." I tend to use it rather than the word "Bible," and, in doing so, I am following a long-standing tradition within Anglicanism. If you look at the texts and rites of the *Book of Common Prayer,* you will find the word "Bible" rarely appears; it is found in only one context, as the name of the *object,* the physical book, that is handed to every newly ordained person at the time of ordination. Otherwise, the Prayer Book talks about "the scriptures"—plural. (For that matter, even the word "Bible" began originally as a plural. It comes from the Greek *ta biblia,* "the scrolls, the books.") Why plural? Because for a thousand years before the Arabs brought paper-making to Europe, it was virtually impossible to collect the whole of the Christian scriptures, Old and New Testament, into a single volume. Papyrus would not hold up to that much folding, and parchment was too stiff and heavy. It was possible to produce a book that could hold all four gospels, say, but a book big enough to hold the whole New Testament was a rarity. When Christians talked about "the scriptures," they were describing the physical reality they knew—books, plural. Even after the introduction of paper, it was mostly scholars who would own a single-volume Bible. Once printing came along these Bibles became more common, but they were still very expensive. The idea of every Christian having a Bible in hand really got underway only in the nineteenth century, when people organized Bible societies to publish them inexpensively and when the invention of pulp paper made the raw material cheaper.

Even though we may assume now that the Bible is a single book, Christians have long read the scriptures not as a single

45

work, but as multiple "writings." And they have read these writings in many different ways. The earliest Christians, of course, had no "New Testament"; they read the scriptures they had—what we now call the "Old Testament" and the "Apocrypha"—as prophecies and foreshadowings of Jesus' life and ministry, mysterious texts that, reread from a new angle, revealed startling, hitherto unsuspected meaning. Think about Paul: he was so confident in his reading of scripture as a young man that he was willing to employ violence against anybody who read it otherwise. Then he found himself confronted by the very person he most detested, the one he marshaled all his texts against—and confronted in such a way as to realize that this Jesus was far more intimate with God than the young Paul could even imagine being (Acts 7:54–8:1; 9:1–19).

After his experience on the way to Damascus (and some reschooling, no doubt, by Christians like Ananias, who cured his blindness), Paul went back to the scriptures and found that they had all along been proclaiming good news not only for Jews but for Gentiles. Paul had never noticed it before! For the earliest Christians, the great thing about the scriptures was their capacity to become new, to speak a word of God that had lain hidden there for generations—for centuries—until it emerged in their own time. Their hope in God opened their eyes, their ears, and their hearts so that God could speak to them afresh out of the ancient texts.

Over the ensuing centuries, Christians read the scriptures for many purposes. They looked to them to explain the meaning of God's incarnation in Jesus and God's presence in the community of the church. They called this the "allegorical" sense of scripture. They also looked for wise counsel about life, which they called the "moral" sense of scripture. And they expected to find in the scriptures the call of God, the invitation to draw near to God, that pulls us toward holiness here and prepares us for heaven (the "anagogical" sense).

Notice that this traditional list does not say much about scripture as a source of rules and laws or even doctrines. It was used in this way at times, but apparently not enough for it to stand out as a distinct purpose or method of reading scripture. The church had confidence in the Spirit to lead it in working these things out as it went along. Even something as basic as the Nicene Creed contains theological language you cannot find in scripture (namely, the statement that Jesus is "of one substance with the Father").

Only in the sixteenth century, with the Reformation, did some Christians begin to argue that the scriptures contain a single, unified theological and moral system. (This probably had a lot to do with the availability of printed Bibles. Now two people in different places could actually read exactly the same text!) For some, like Martin Luther, this was a matter of finding the *heart* of the gospel and then working out its theological implications. He even felt free to reject certain biblical passages in the light of this central message. For others, notably John Calvin, biblical interpretation took a more detailed and systematic form. When you know that Luther was a theologian by profession and Calvin a lawyer, you will begin to grasp some of the differences in their approach. Luther wanted first principles; Calvin wanted specifics.

And Anglicans—what did our Reformation ancestors do with all this? Ah, here we are getting to the point! Anglican reformers shared the other reformers' basic concerns and hopes for the church and Christian faith. Like Lutherans and Calvinists, Anglicans saw that the scriptures challenged some of the developments that had shaped late medieval Christianity. And, like them, we used scripture as a kind of pruning hook to remove a lot of usages that had grown up like suckers, obscuring the main trunk of the tree of Christian faith: ideas of the Eucharist, for example, that verged on the magical; a cult of saints that sometimes threatened to usurp the place of Jesus; and an insistence on celibacy that made the holiness of married people irrelevant.

There were Anglicans, early on, who would have liked to go further and subscribe to the full Calvinist or Lutheran system; and there were others who really rather detested the whole Reformation. But those who were guiding the church did not take either direction. Instead, they fell back on a very ancient practice that did not presume anything, one way or the other, about the scriptures as a theological system. They built the scriptures into the worship of the church—particularly the Daily Offices of Morning and Evening Prayer.

These daily services of prayer and the reading of the scriptures became the most common experience of worship for Reformation and post-Reformation Anglicans. The Eucharist was celebrated less frequently then than it is today because people were reluctant to receive communion for fear of eating and drinking damnation to themselves (cf. 1 Cor. 11:27–34), and the reformers did not want the Eucharist to be celebrated without the people receiving communion. When our forebears worshipped, then, they did so with the reading of massive—some might say "indigestible"—quantities of scripture. This stood in contrast with the Puritan inclination to read only a short passage, a few verses that would then be expounded in a sermon. As every Anglican preacher knows, it is hardly ever possible to preach from all the texts the lectionary has assigned to a particular service. The point for us was not to have the scriptures *explained* at the heart of worship, but rather to have the scriptures *heard* and left relatively free to communicate with the worshippers.

This pushed us, right from the start, toward a way of reading scripture that was different from other strands of Western Christianity. Others concentrated on expounding doctrine and morals. Anglicans did plenty of that, too, in other contexts. But, in worship, we were just thrown into the deep end of the scriptural pool and told to swim for it. We were expected to make sense of it as we went—and pray at the same time! In the process, we sometimes encounter some very strange assortments of readings, coupled together merely by chance as we make our way through the chapters of each book, and not with any particular theme in mind. Take, for example, these lectionary readings for one particular autumn day, using the Daily Office lectionary in the 1979 American *Book of Common Prayer*.[22]

> *Psalm 31:* "In you, O LORD, have I taken refuge..." (v. 1). This psalm is a lament, alternating between confidence in God and complaint about the singer's terrible situation.

> *Ecclesiasticus 11:2–20:* This book from the Apocrypha, also known as Sirach, is largely a compilation of traditional wisdom, and for this reason is full of good advice, much of it still applicable. "Do not praise individuals for

their good looks, or loath anyone because of appearance alone" (v. 2); "Do not boast about wearing fine clothes, and do not exalt yourself when you are honored" (v. 4).

Revelation 9:13–21: Here we are plunged into a vivid apocalyptic vision in which a third of humanity is killed. Still, the evil do not turn away from their idolatry and sin.

Luke 10:38–42: We finish with the story of Mary and Martha, where Mary chooses to sit at Jesus' feet with the men and listen, while Martha is doing double duty to put dinner together. Who can wonder that Martha complains? And why does Jesus take Mary's side?

What is a person to do? How do we make any sense of these texts, much less pray with them? It is enough to produce a case of spiritual whiplash. And it is easy to understand why Puritans preferred a sermon with one or two points and a short list of texts to "prove" them. But, friends and readers, *this* is what the scriptures are really like. They are not simple. They are not systematic. They are not even clearly organized. They were never meant to answer all our questions. Sometimes, their most important gift is to give us new ones.

The psalm here sets a standard of honesty in prayer. The psalmist has a problem of faith—and feels no problem in saying so! It is a psalm for those times when God does not seem to be doing too well by us. But the psalmist is still praying, nudging, insisting. The Psalms are full of such subversive models of prayer, and for centuries Anglicans have learned from them how to pray honestly. If a given psalm happens to match your needs the day it comes up in the readings, well and good. If not, learn from it how to proceed in other times, when life demands a different sort of prayer.

Sirach, by contrast, is in love with the coolness of reason and moderation. Maybe his life was not as conflicted as that of the psalmist. But even the psalmist could probably have seen Sirach's life of prudence and moderation and good sense as a kind of goal, a deliverance from the present anxiety. It gives one something to aim at, at least. It offers a model of maturity and civic responsibility that, for the most part, is as useful as ever.

The Revelation to John speaks to a completely different situation, one where there is no hope at all for this world short of immediate and devastating divine intervention. The visions are so vivid and powerful that they lay hold of the imagination whether we want them to or not. Perhaps Sirach could have turned a deaf ear to them or dismissed them as too emotional and exaggerated. But many other people of faith have found that impossible. Our early reformers actually kept Revelation *out* of the Daily Office lectionary. They apparently feared it would have a bad influence on the general public; and, to judge by recent fascination with apocalyptic matters, they may have been right. But, still, there are moments in human existence when nothing less passionate can capture the reality people are actually living through. The obscenity (I think that is a legitimate term here) of the modern fascination with Revelation is that its proponents are so often people who are actually pretty well off, sitting in comfortable houses and churches and aiming their anger and hatred at the rest of the world. They probably would not like Sirach's advice much; and Sirach might not think highly of their religion.

Then we get to the passage from Luke. The story of Mary and Martha has been used in various ways: to prove that the contemplative life is better than the active life; to belittle the value of what was traditionally women's work; to exalt the importance of education. The thing that jumped out for me in my most recent traversal of these passages is the way Jesus repeats Martha's name in addressing her: "Martha, Martha." This is what he does in Luke's gospel when he wants someone to take him very seriously. But what is he telling her? Maybe he's saying to her, "Be at ease. I am an easier guest than you imagined." Or maybe he's saying, "I came to *see you,* not for the feast." Mary is not to be limited to predefined gender roles. But Martha's ministry is not therefore devalued. She is invited to offer what she can, not enslave herself to some standard beyond her ability to provide.

There is no simple way to put all these texts together, and in fact coming up with a single theme for these diverse readings in the lectionary is not even the point. How we understand them and how we pray with them—or through, or around, or even despite them—will vary not only from person to person, but from one part or time of your life to another. It is this openness with scripture, this expectation that God will speak a living Word to us through the words we hear, that is characteristic of the Anglican approach to reading the scriptures. We did not invent this practice. It comes straight out of the earliest church's understanding of scripture as a living Word of God, with the expectation that God can and will meet us through these pages—not necessarily in the surface meaning, and probably in ways that will surprise us, but effectively nonetheless. Reading the scriptures in the context of daily prayer, with an openness to hearing what God has to say to us today, is an ancient practice, but in modern Western Christianity it has found a particular home among Anglicans.

We expect to find God speaking to us in scripture, and we do find God speaking to us in scripture. But, at the same time, we accept the reality that scripture is a vast and confusing set of texts, some of which, at any given moment, may seem unintelligible or unhelpful—at worst, even wrong-headed. W. H. Auden summed up this Anglican way with scripture in a short poem from his Christmas oratorio, called "For the Time Being." He describes God's word in scripture as written by human hands in "a smudged and crooked line" and yet remaining, for all that, "legible."[23] The word of God in scripture comes not like a fast-food hamburger, neatly packaged, but like assorted vegetables straight from the garden, requiring some cleaning, some chewing, and some time for digestion.

This is not a trivial matter. The way we read the scriptures is closely related to how we see not only God, but also the world and ourselves; religious formation is pervasive and powerful. It would seem that it is also difficult to alter, as Lorenza Colzato and her colleagues at the Leiden Institute for Brain and Cognition have confirmed. When they tested the bias of seventy-two Dutch Christian and atheist participants toward either global or local processing, clear differences emerged between the life-long atheists, who showed the strongest bias for the big picture, followed by the liberal Calvinists, and then by the conservative Calvinists and conservative Calvinists-turned-atheists, who showed an equivalently strong bias for small details. "The latter two groups performed similarly," the blog report noted, "suggesting that more than seven years without religious practice wasn't enough to remove the effects of the religion on a person's attentional mindset."[24]

Now, the world needs both big-picture people and detail people. It also needs people who can do some of each. And that, I think, is something our peculiarly Anglican way of dealing with scripture has been good at. It stands in sharp contrast with efforts to use the Bible as the authority for a highly detailed and articulated theological and moral system, which lies at the root of some perennial conflicts within Anglicanism itself. We have, after all, both Catholic and Puritan (Calvinist) heritages. The Puritan interpretation of scripture excelled at giving clear directions, though the biblical foundation for them was often less secure than was claimed. But it militated against the possibility of surprise emerging from the pages of scripture. At its worst, the Puritan Bible is scripture in a strait-jacket, forced to reside within very strict limits and behave itself. Great claims can then be made for it, claims to infallibility or inerrancy. Some of their contemporaries accused the Puritans of having created a "paper pope." Roman Catholics didn't need a paper pope, since they had a real one. But both groups made sure that the Bible would always agree with them.

The Anglican approach to the Bible has not been as useful at answering questions and it does demand a lot more work on the part of the reader. But it also leaves a lot of room to be surprised by grace. It puts us in the way of God's gifts. Some of the readings will prove useless to you at any given moment in your life. Some of them will show you grace from the first moment you hear them. Some of them will suggest to you possibilities you would never have thought of on your own. Sometimes, you will find God intervening to speak quite directly to your own life.

This is the historic legacy our Reformation forebears left us. This way of understanding the Bible is not the same thing as modern Christian liberalism, even though it may overlap with it at times. The point is not to dismiss the literal meaning of the text, much less to minimize the value of scripture, but to allow the full complexity of scripture to surface. The process allows scripture to become deeper and more radiant, even to lift us into God's presence in worship.

But this sort of reading does demand attention. It takes extensive engagement with the texts precisely in the context of common prayer, where there is no time or encouragement to spend your energy making the texts agree with one another. Instead, you are bringing them into direct contact with the life of the moment, your own and that of the communities of which you are a part: your family, your church, your city, your nation, the world at large.

I am concerned that knowledge of the Bible may be a place where our tradition has grown rather weak. We need a significant revival of reading and studying scripture in the context of prayer and of the life of the Spirit, and we do see some beginnings of this. The ancient Benedictine practice of *lectio divina* has many practitioners again. The use of the African Bible Study method has helped many people discover the importance of sharing diverse insights. But, given the relative loss of the Daily Office in our world—a world where complex calendars make community events difficult—we probably need to be finding additional ways for this kind of reading to soak into people's minds and hearts.

It takes a lifetime, for most of us, for the good news of Jesus really to penetrate our hearts and souls, to shape us in trust and hope and love. If we are not yet perfect in these three, then we should expect to be surprised again by God's grace in the future. Indeed, when we begin to suspect that we might be pretty well formed in our Christian faith, we are probably just setting ourselves up for a new surprise.

Sacrament and scripture. These are the gifts that have shaped Anglicanism in the past. We have found God meeting us, challenging us, confronting us through both of these means. This does not mean that the future will hold no surprises. We have passed through major changes in our common worship over the last century or so. We have gone from infrequent to frequent communion, from private to public baptism. We have embraced, not always with delight, new lectionaries and new translations of scripture. We have discovered more than once that our reading of scripture has been incomplete, inadequate, or just plain wrong. Openness to this kind of change is a gift, not a problem. We may have to discover new ways of fostering all these gifts and sharing them. But I do not think we will ever abandon either the sacraments or the scriptures, because they do indeed lift us into the presence of their Giver.

> O God of peace, who hast taught us that in returning and rest we shall be saved, in quietness and in confidence shall be our strength: By the might of thy Spirit lift us, we pray thee, to thy presence, where we may be still and know that thou art God; through Jesus Christ our Lord. *Amen.*

4

BEING THE COMMUNION
OF SAINTS

In this chapter, we turn our attention to a third aspect of our
peculiarity as Anglicans. Perhaps I should say "particular-
ity"—a nicer word! And yet, there is something to be said for
the slightly archaic "peculiarity." It's a bit like "eccentricity,"
for which we have always had a soft spot. And it has the
merit of making no claim for our own virtue—the merit, in
other words, of humility. After all, every gift of the Spirit is
exactly that—a gift, not a badge of merit or a bit of private
property to be shown off, bragged about, and used as one
pleases. This third aspect is our focus on the community of
faith, or communion of saints. I use the phrase "communion
of saints" to emphasize that this community is characterized
by something different from generalized niceness, or the im-
position of uniformity, or bored tolerance, or clubbiness. It
may, at times, degenerate into one or another of those things;
but, in itself, it is something quite different. The communion
of saints is an attitude that finds the heart of the church in
the *community* of people being drawn to the gospel and
transformed by it—not in doctrines, not in a particular hier-
archy, not in a pope (whether human or on paper), not in a
uniform ethical understanding, but in the community itself.

In a way, this makes us a bit like our cousins in faith, the
Jewish people. Over the years, I have heard this observation
from more than one Jewish friend. Our strong commitment
to the community can accommodate a great deal of disagree-
ment, not unlike what is typical of Judaism. Sometimes we
glory in this capacity. Sometimes we grow very weary of it.

Some of us even try to overturn it. But it has survived a very long time among us. It, too, deserves to be considered one of our fundamental gifts, one of the treasures of grace that we must seek to carry forward with us into the future.

The community of holy ones

What do we mean by "the communion of saints"? We confess our belief in it through the Apostles' Creed. The original Latin is ambiguous, and scholars have suggested that the phrase originally meant something more like "the sharing of holy things," probably with a sacramental reference. I am using it here, though, in the sense that has become familiar to us, "the community of holy ones"—not only human saints, but also the holy angels whom we celebrate and in whose prayer we join. What does it mean to "believe" in this communion and to be a part of it?

We could begin with the properly certified saints, the "big haloes," the ones with the honorific in front of their names, the ones who appear in our various calendars. But I propose to start at a different point in order to guard against the whole notion becoming too formal and distant. Think, if you will, about the saints who have shaped your own life. The saints I have in mind are pretty ordinary people, for the most part, not so different from the rest of us. They are people you have known at different times in your life. They are people through whom you glimpsed something of goodness, something of God. Someone with a ready laugh who taught you delight in the world. Someone with a gift of attention who took you seriously when you may not have taken yourself seriously. Someone who just liked you and showed you by that generous affirmation what grace is. Someone who pulled you up short but without rancor, just because somebody needed to say "Whoa!" Somebody who took you fishing. Somebody who let you borrow books from her library.

At first, these may not seem like saints at all. They do not seem *different* enough from the rest of us, do they? They probably were not particularly heroic or ascetic or single-minded. But that's exactly the point I want to make. Being a saint isn't primarily about being a great figure. Being a saint is primarily about letting some ray of the light of God through, whether intentionally or, quite often, without so much as thinking of it.

How did you come to be aware of the love of God? There's no single answer to that. Each of us has had distinct experiences of it. But woven all through that process is the work and witness of saints: people we crossed paths with who showed us that pervading all of creation is a generosity that we have not earned or deserved, but that somehow goes with us from day to day. I say "people," but the communion of saints is not limited to human beings. Christians have always numbered the angels among the saints, and I will suggest later on that other created orders may be saints to us, too.

To some extent, all of us in the Western world are self-made or at least self-defined persons. That idea has come in for a lot of abuse—and justly so. It is absurd on the face of it, and it can become an excuse for extreme selfishness. If you really can imagine that you have made yourself from the ground up, then you don't owe anybody anything, right? You can behave with complete selfish regard and feel righteous about it.

Still, we do live in a culture that gives us a substantial amount of choice in our lives. With it goes the responsibility of constructing a life of sense and integrity instead of simply imitating what others do. Each of us really does have to be "self-made" in a certain sense. But from earliest childhood onward, we are always picking up signals from the people around us. Some of them are signals of repression and discouragement, some of them signals of encouragement and love. People show us examples of all the big vices and all the big virtues and, to a great degree, leave us to sort them out ourselves. As we learn to make sense out of all these sometimes conflicting signals we see that some ways of life build steady and generous people who know something about delight, while some other ways of life get people into situations where they bring suffering on themselves and others.

And so we have made choices, built lives, worked in the cracks and crevices, and taken up the opportunities that our world provided. We have worked partly out of our own deep-rooted being, discovering as we grew up that each of us is a new and unsuspected manifestation of what it is to be human. We have worked sometimes out of fear and self-protection. And sometimes we have worked out of hope and with the strength of God's grace, the generosity of God's love—and we have learned how to do that, often as not, from these saints all around us.

I do not mean to *restrict* our knowledge of God's love to this one source, our experience of life in the community of saints. We learn about God from the scriptures. We learn to know God in the sacraments. And some of us have had very direct, personal encounters with God—what people often call "mystical" experience. (Perhaps not everybody does—or at least not everybody is conscious of it. But many people do.) But however else we get acquainted with God, we also depend on our saints.

Even having a word for "love" and knowing what it means comes from the people among whom we have lived and grown up. How could we know what it means to say "God is love" (1 John 4:8), if we had not first had some glimpse of love around us? Of course, we have also learned the opposite of love from other people. That just makes our saints all the more important for us.

I hope this rambling and allusive discussion may be sparking memories of some of your own saints. Who has conveyed some of God's grace and generosity in your life? I can tell you about a few of mine.

I think of one of my aunts: my mother's favorite sister, I think. She kept an eye out for one of her nephews and offered a kind of quiet and undemanding love that gave me a sense of belonging in a large and sometimes bewildering family. She married late in life and then lost her husband to cancer after only a few years. Despite that sorrow, she never seemed to lose her quiet, unforced affection.

I think of my brother, seven years older than I, who made sure that I grew up with wider horizons than my family might otherwise have provided.

I think of senior colleagues I worked with over the years who had the gift of putting our academic work in larger, more humane perspective. They helped me find focus as a teacher and a scholar without shutting myself up in what can sometimes turn out to be a kind of academic ghetto, cut off from the rest of life.

I think of a gardener friend, from whom I learned not only a great deal about plants and landscaping, but the wisdom to admit that every garden is an experimental garden. That insight has served me well in many areas of life. Sometimes it even helps me avoid attaching more importance to my efforts than they deserve.

I think of a fellow priest who was an "out" lesbian long before Stonewall and had an amazing trust in God. She knew that she could expect God to engage with her in her life and that the results were likely to be both significant and comical at the same time.

I think of a Hawaiian laywoman whom I came to know while she was a trustee of the Church Divinity School of the Pacific. She had the generosity and patience to see me through a crisis at work that nobody else quite seemed to understand at the time.

None of these people were perfect. My aunt had some of the rigidities of her place and time. My gardening friend succumbed to alcohol and abandoned the people who had known him longest. But each of them gave gifts—gifts that helped me come to know God and to know myself better in God's presence.

People like these have helped shape all our lives. Sometimes they have held us back from mistakes. Sometimes they have given us hope when things looked grim. They have reminded us that the most powerful force in our world isn't money or popularity or political power, but love. Love can transform and create and build. The other powers of this world too often just shove things around or even tear them apart.

Whoever your personal saints may be, I invite you to hold them in thought just now as we turn to a classic prayer that celebrates the communion of saints:

Almighty God, you have knit together your elect in one communion and fellowship in the mystical body of your Son Christ our Lord: Give us grace so to follow

your blessed saints in all virtuous and godly living, that
we may come to those ineffable joys that you have prepared for those who truly love you; through Jesus
Christ our Lord, who with you and the Holy Spirit
lives and reigns, one God, in glory everlasting. *Amen.*[25]

Being numbered with the saints

"Virtuous and godly living" may sound narrow, rigid, even
rather depressing. But remember that it is aimed at "ineffable
joys." The saints taken as a whole cannot be a drab and joy-
less lot. There is a well-known jazz song from New Orleans
called "Oh when the saints go marching in" that includes the
line, "I want to be in that number," which expresses an age-
old Christian longing. I would guess that the sentiment came
right out of the *Te deum*: "Make us to be numbered with thy
saints." And these beloved and wise friends or colleagues
with whom we live and work are the saints with whom we
want to be numbered. All those formal saints, the ones who
have the capitalized "St." in front of their names—they are
an odd assortment, and not all of them were people you
would look forward to having a glass of wine and dinner
with.

Jesus himself had a reputation for being good company at
parties. People kept inviting him back, which tells us a great
deal. Sometimes, with a little prompting from his mother, he
even brought the wine. But we are apt to think of those
"Saint" people with a capital *S* as another breed altogether.
They were pretty single-minded, maybe not very good con-
versationalists. Some of them were very ascetic and we wonder if they will look disapprovingly at the food we have
served. Others locked themselves up in hermitages—so probably they would not accept your invitation anyway!

Some, like Benedict, were very hospitable or, like Francis,
immensely generous to everybody with their time and attention. But with a good many of them you get the feeling that
they did not like other human beings all that much. Some
were very censorious; some were pretty angry people. Some
even preached crusades or defended the Inquisition. I do not

mean to exile them from the communion of saints, but I am thinking here about the saints you can imagine having a fine time with over dinner. In fact, you probably *have* had a fine time over dinner with some of them. The others are welcome, too, but these are the ones who are most intimately connected with our lives, who have played and continue to play a central role in encouraging faith, strengthening hope, evoking love.

Believing in the communion of saints means—for one thing—recognizing that we are never isolated. Even when we are alone, we are part of this community. We have all been formed, in so many ways, by the people around us. We carry with us bits and pieces of their influence, reshaped and fitted into our own emerging psyches and personalities. We are heirs of those who went before, kin of our kin, friends of our friends. Much of what is good and grace-filled in us—the "virtuous and godly living" that leads to "ineffable joys"— we have received from them. In emphasizing these personal saints, the ones we have known directly, I hope we can rescue the communion of saints from overinflated expectations and reclaim its essential value in our lives.

It may well be that some of the saints from whom you have learned much are in fact people you know because of their great reputation, not from personal acquaintance. They belong to the category of the "great saints." You know them from stories about them: St. Francis befriending the wolf, maybe, or preaching to the birds; Dorothy Day committing herself to the service of the poor and oppressed; Rosa Parks finding the courage to claim her place as the equal of her oppressors; Dietrich Bonhoeffer searching for a way to be a responsible citizen in a violent world.

Or you may know them through their writings. Think of all those great hymns by Charles Wesley: "Jesus, Lover of my soul," "Love divine, all loves excelling," "O for a thousand tongues to sing." Or Madeleine L'Engle's novels. Or Brother Lawrence's *Practice of the Presence of God.* Or Martin Luther King, Jr.'s powerful speeches. I would certainly have to number George Herbert, Henry Vaughan, Thomas Traherne, and Christina Rossetti among my personal saints.

The Epistle to the Hebrews says that we are surrounded by a great cloud of witnesses (12:1). It is mind-boggling, in fact, to think back beyond our immediate saints to the thousands of years that shaped them and us, to people who were living the life of faith and hope and love before any of us was born.

And you know something? None of those historic saints was perfect, either—not even the official ones with the "St." in front of their names. Think of St. Columba, missionary to the Scots and Picts (not to mention being the first person recorded as having seen the Loch Ness monster). Do you know why he left Ireland and founded Iona? It was an act of penance. He had been a very holy and learned monk at home. But he borrowed a book from another monastery and copied it without their permission. When they found out, they claimed the copy and he refused. The dispute wound up in the courts, which ruled that the calf goes with the cow, the copy with the source; but he refused to give it up. He was so angry that he sparked a battle between the two monasteries, which also meant, in effect, a civil war between two branches of his own family, the O'Neils. God still knew how to make use of him. The formal saints are important to us for the same reason our more private saints are important: they transmitted some of God's light. And sometimes it was their flaws, their mistakes, their inadequacies, in fact, that allowed God access to them and, through them, to us.

We have a great chain of saints, a great chain of holiness, that extends far back into the dawn of human existence: Enoch, for example, so intimate with God that when it came time for him to die he simply "was no more, for God took him" (Gen. 5:24). And their successors are still with us, still opening up the possibilities of God's love for us to discover and take hold of and live out. The communion of saints includes the formal, official saints. It includes our personal saints. And when we profess faith in the communion of saints, we are acknowledging that we want to be in that number, too.

Now, you may be thinking that some of your personal saints were not church people, were not Christians. Yes, that's all right. We tend to think of the communion of saints primarily in terms of our forebears in Israel and in the church: Abraham and Sarah, Moses, the prophets, the sages of Israel, the apostles and martyrs, champions of the poor and the sick, educators, poets, mystics, the whole amazing array of the saints—including multitudes of unsung saints whose lives changed their families, their friends, their communities for the good. But we shouldn't draw too tight a line around this communion of saints. God has never said to us, "You are mine, but I refuse to have anything to do with all those people outside." No! The Spirit is always at work, anywhere and everywhere, "unresting, unhasting, and silent as light," as the hymn says.[26] Remember the story in Luke's Gospel (7:1–10) where a Roman army officer sends to Jesus asking him to heal his slave. And Jesus says of him, "Not even in Israel have I found such faith." An outsider can be a saint too. In fact, since holiness is the *gift* of God, sometimes outsiders may convey it better than insiders. We do not ever want to forget that. The faith of Israel and of the church provides a *home* for the communion of saints. It does not *monopolize* it.

Still, we give thanks that we can rejoice in this long history of grace, this family of saints, insiders and outsiders, to which we belong. We give thanks that we can form another link in it. For make no mistake: we are not the last generation. God is not done with this world. We are joint heirs with those who went before us and we are custodians of a treasure that we can and will pass on to others.

A larger company of saints

And we can enlarge our company of saints further. For many of us, nature has provided an important window on God. I would say it is a major feature of spirituality for great numbers of people in our world. In the United States, the principal "pilgrimage centers" are the great national parks like the Grand Canyon, Yosemite, Yellowstone. We Christians have been a little unsure how to acknowledge this reverence for the beauty of the natural world in relation to our faith, even though we, too, are drawn to these places. Where does Jesus come into it, after all?

The first part of the answer is clear enough. The first article of the creeds proclaims that God is the creator of all this wonder and beauty. And, from the very beginning, Christians have spoken of Jesus as the agent of this creation: Jesus is the Wisdom of creation; Jesus is the Logos, the Word of creation; Jesus is the Goal of creation. It is right there in the Nicene Creed as well as in such New Testament texts as the Gospel of John (1:1–18) and the Epistle to the Hebrews (1:1–4).

To honor the creation is a way to honor the creator. And the creation also teaches us something of the creator that we could learn in no other way. In the famous words of Gerard Manley Hopkins:

> The world is charged with the grandeur of God.
> It will flame out, like shining from shook foil.... [27]

And the splendor we encounter in a place like Yosemite, reminds us to notice God's hand in humbler circumstances, too: early morning light on the trees of a neighbor's garden, a pot of bulbs in flower at a gray time of year, the surprise of seeds sprouting.

Our communion of saints has always extended beyond the human community to embrace the angels: Michael, the protector of the faithful, Gabriel, bringer of good news, the cherubim and seraphim who lead the worship of the whole creation, the great unseen array. You may think of angels as being categorically different from the Grand Canyon or Old Faithful. Aren't they supposed to be supernatural? But they, too, are part of the created order, along with the seas and the dry land, the plants, the animals, the stars, and us human beings. The psalmist didn't draw all that sharp a distinction between angels and the rest of creation. As an older Prayer Book translation had it:

> [God] maketh his angels winds
> and his ministers a flaming fire. (Ps. 104:4)[28]

The words in Hebrew and Greek that we translate as "angel" actually mean "messenger." God employs many kinds of messengers, and the psalmist does not seem to see any absolute difference among them.

So enlarge your sense of "angels," if you will. Or, at any rate, your sense of being in communion with the creation at large. This is nothing new, actually, though we have tended to lose sight of this part of our tradition. As Anglicans have shifted, over the past hundred years, to treating the Eucharist as our central form of Sunday worship, many of us no longer know the canticles that are part of Morning and Evening Prayer. But the *Benedicite* is an appeal to all creation to join us in praise:

> O all ye works of the Lord, bless ye the Lord;
> praise him and magnify him for ever.

> O ye angels of the Lord, bless ye the Lord;
> praise him and magnify him for ever.

> ......

> O ye sun and moon, bless ye the Lord;
> O ye stars of heaven, bless ye the Lord;

> O ye showers and dew, bless ye the Lord:
> praise him and magnify him for ever.[29]

And the list goes on through winter and summer, frost and cold, nights and days, lightnings and clouds, mountains and hills, all green things upon the earth, wells, seas, whales, birds, beasts and cattle, and, yes, humanity.

We have been through a couple of centuries when human beings (perhaps especially Western human beings) have behaved as if the world were just a piece of abandoned real estate to be divided up and turned to some kind of profit. Now we are being forced to recognize that we actually have a vast and complex interdependency with this world where we live. What we thought of as something we could freely dispose of, it now turns out, just might wind up disposing of us.

There is a prudential side to the contemporary renewal of concern about ecology, about the health and well-being of the whole earth. But there is also a spiritual side to it. It has been implicit for a long time in the setting aside of national parks and, for that matter, public parks and gardens of all sorts. Now we see it reemerging also in a reverence for wilderness (the place our ancient forebears went when they particularly needed to talk with God), in the defense of endangered species, or in the search for sustainable modes of agriculture.

Some of this (by no means all) is coming from people of strong Christian sensibilities. Whoever it comes from, it represents respect and even reverence for the created order, the same kind of awareness of possibility, of God's grace shining through, that Gerald Manley Hopkins and the psalmist both wrote about.

These messengers, these angels of God, belong in our communion of saints, too. They are our companions along with our human saints—something that Jesus exemplified when, after being tempted by Satan, he found refuge and restoration with the angels and "the wild beasts" (Mark 1:13). The natural world is not just a piece of undervalued real estate—nor is it simply a derelict case that we, in our eagerness to do good, have to take care of. It is our companion, our elder sister and brother, a whole communion of angelic messengers with warnings to share and also news of God's goodness and greatness.

The communion of saints and the church

So, we have our human saints, some of them on the official calendar, most of them probably not. (The unofficial ones may be more effective than the official ones at shaping our lives.) And we also have this array of beings from other orders of creation—angels, the natural world. The communion of saints is a very rich community to live in!

And there's one more dimension to our Christian thinking about saints that we also need to look at. You may remember that when Paul wrote letters to people, he routinely addressed them as "the *saints* who are in Corinth"—or Thessalonica or Philippi or wherever.

What he meant by that was to say that we are *all* holy (the root meaning of the word "saint"). Now, how did we become "holy"? It was not by being heroic. You might wind up being heroic *because* you are holy, but it's not a prerequisite. We are holy, in Paul's thinking, because we belong to God, because God has laid claim to us and we have accepted the claim.

Paul, when he wrote to the "holy ones at Corinth," was not limiting his audience to, say, clergy or professional church workers. He was writing to everyone there. He was taking it for granted that they had been claimed by God and that they had consented to that and understood themselves that way, that they had experienced the grace of God and were at least beginning to be a bit transparent to it.

Now, you might think that Paul had a better grade of Christians in congregations like Corinth than we personally find in the average modern congregation. But you would be very wrong. If you really want to hang onto that explanation, make very, very sure that you never actually *read* the letters. Were Paul's converts a particularly high class of devout Christians? No. Paul spends a big part of the letters telling his saints that they have not really got the idea yet or, if they have, they are not doing a great job of carrying it out.

Those people gossiped, formed factions, got into fights with each other, took each other to court, argued about who was in charge, wandered off in search of new excitement, got drunk, got brought up on morals charges, were stingy with their offerings for the poor, scared themselves with worries about the end of the world.... If Paul's converts had not been such a headache, he probably would not have written very many letters.

He still calls them "saints." He still thinks this is the right name for them. And apparently the same conditions apply to us, too. So we need to think some more about what kind of holiness this is that can make itself known through us even when we are not paying full attention, even when we may be fighting it.

I like the people I go to church with in Berkeley. But I confess I, too, have a hard time thinking of us, myself included, as saints. Probably any one of us could begin a sentence with the words, "Well, I'm no saint, but.... " And Paul would say, "Oy! two thousand years and they still don't get it!"

And yet, our sainthood is real. It is real because it is not, first and foremost, about how good we are. It's about how good God is. And, I might add, how sneaky God can be. When you live around the scriptures and the sacraments, when you take part in the prayers and praises of the community, when you belong to a group of people that may well include one or two of your own personal saints, you begin to pick things up. You begin to start behaving more like them.

It's a bit like citizenship, isn't it? How do you learn to be a good citizen? You may have had a bit of training in it, in a civics class or in a course for new citizens. But you mostly learn by doing. You learn by paying attention year in and year out, by figuring out how to weigh political advertisements, by voting, by sitting on juries, by responding to public need. And you begin to notice that you didn't invent this citizenship. It's a gift from your forebears—and a gift that you, too, have to pass on.

Sainthood is like that. You have the benefit of your own saints who have helped you catch glimpses of God's grace in a human life. Now you are in the process, whether you are fully conscious of it or not, of becoming a saint for some other people.

Remember, it does not require perfection. Good thing, too! Have there ever been any saints who have been perfect? Sometimes, Francis seems close to it, but I'll bet he would have denied it emphatically. Sometimes the greatest, holiest gift we have to give is the chance for people to see how God's grace can follow even upon our worst mistakes.

When Paul addresses us as "saints," then, he is not saying, "You lovely, sweet, innocent, gracious, virtuous, noble, heroic people!" He's saying, "You lot are an awful mess, but you belong to God and to this community. Get over yourselves and see if you can figure out how to be sources of hope and joy in it instead of a constant drain on the rest of us."

It's not asking so very much, is it? Well, sometimes it seems like it is asking quite a lot, especially when it involves having to work with one of your less cooperative fellow saints. But, in the great scheme of things, no, it's not so very much to ask.

There is a tricky element to it, of course. The Spirit is inclined to be tricky. There is a hymn "I sing a song of the saints of God," written for children, though it has a broad following among adults, too.[30] It makes the saints sound rather cozy at first: "One was a doctor, and one was a queen, and one was a shepherdess on the green...." I particularly like the part that comes further on: "You can meet them in school, or in lanes, or at sea, in church, or in trains, or in shops, or at tea...." It's that bit about meeting them at tea that catches me, since I'm basically devoted to meals and the good things that can happen when people are enjoying food and company around a table.

And it is no contradiction to note that some of the people lurking behind those descriptions also went on to live lives of heroic sanctity: doctors who risked their lives to save others; queens who saw the distress of the poor and left their palace life to go and help. That shepherdess on the green was St. Genevieve, patron of Paris, who lived a life of austerity and prayer, worked miracles, and was said to have saved Paris from the armies of Attila partly through her prayers and partly by figuring out how to bring provisions in by the river. Tea with any of these folk would be a high-powered occasion.

There is indeed a continuity between our everyday saints and those saints who have become heroes. And if God needs you for that kind of sainthood, God will let you know. You probably cannot escape by lying low, in any case. In the meantime, this more ordinary sainthood, this sainthood that has shaped each of us and sustained each of us through our lives, this sainthood by which we ourselves shape and sustain others—this is nothing to be scoffed at. This is the warp and woof of the fabric of human community, the fabric of human life. This is where everyday human reality lives and breathes. And God is here. God is at work among us. The Spirit never stops breezing through us like the wind, never stops breathing new life through each one of us into our neighbor.

Does this sound familiar? Sometimes we forget because daily existence gets the better of us and we get so wrapped up in current needs and wants and disputes and uncertainties. And God knows that there are plenty of current needs and wants to tend to! These are not the safest or the happiest of times. But we still know the value of this communion of saints, the community of giving and receiving. Without it, there would be few Anglicans—perhaps few Christians of any sort—left in the world, I think.

Yes, the church

I started off talking about the communion of saints. And I have wound up talking about the church. The church may not be exactly the same thing as the communion of saints. But it is its witness, its image, its anchor, its sacrament in the world, in this visible and tangible universe. So, to be serious about being part of the communion of saints means getting serious about the church.

We have not been in a mood to praise the church lately. We are in a time of conflict—big, public conflict. We are confronting the reality of some shameful wrong-doings in the church's past. We cannot just forget the problems or walk away from them. But the time has also come to remember just how important the church is and what a gift from God it can be: the most visible, tangible manifestation there is of the ongoing communion of the saints.

Remember this: Jesus wrote no books. But he did form a community of disciples. He put it together using people who must have disliked each other and regarded one another with suspicion.

> They weren't self-selected,
> would never have formed a team
> on their own initiative. Peter
> was always out front, falling
> on his face; Simon the Zealot
> standing at the edge, waiting
> to catch another fault
> in his less pious brethren.
> Andrew and Philip were doers,
> trying to get on with the business
> of the day, if only they could learn
> what it was. Thomas,
> always perplexed. Judas
> Iscariot, the one who could keep score
> and therefore held the ministry
> of the exchequer. Matthew, the reformed
> tax-collector, never fully
> trusted by the rest. As odd

an assortment as one's own family
or the people where one works.[31]

Yet, these folk—all but Judas—were transformed, bit by bit, as they endeavored to embrace and share the gifts they were given. They acquired an ability to help in the transformation of others. They joined the communion of saints already populated by the likes of Enoch and Abraham, of Isaiah and Amos, of David the king and Job the outsider, who wasn't even an Israelite. They witnessed to God's grace alongside the angels and the natural world. This communion of saints is broader than the church, but it is nonetheless manifest in the church, which exists, really, only to point to God's grace emerging through the communion of saints. This communion is for ever under construction in each succeeding age, as generation succeeds generation. Here we find help to discover our own unique calling; and here we have the opportunity to contribute to the life of others.

So welcome all the saints. Welcome all your personal saints. Welcome the "big haloes." Welcome the angels. Welcome all the creatures of the place where you find yourself. And step into your own place in the chorus as we celebrate the God who made us and loves us. This communion of saints is not just a gift we have received. It is a gift we *are*. This is why we bear with our differences, even when we disagree, even when we get quite angry with one another. And it is difficult to imagine anything that would give the world around us more hope than to see this kind of community flourishing in its midst.

> Almighty God, you have knit together your elect in one communion and fellowship in the mystical body of your Son Christ our Lord: Give us grace so to follow your blessed saints in all virtuous and godly living, that we may come to those ineffable joys that you have prepared for those who truly love you; through Jesus Christ our Lord, who with you and the Holy Spirit lives and reigns, one God, in glory everlasting. *Amen.*

5

REDISCOVERING HUMILITY

I have been praising some of the good things we have received through our Anglican tradition. We have particularly noted the gift of a life shaped by the sacraments, a way of worship that takes our whole humanity seriously and allows God's grace into the midst of it. And we have considered the gift of scriptures read in the context of prayer—a way of reading that is both ancient and still very much alive, a way of reading them that acknowledges their strangeness, their mystery, and also their power to open unexpected pathways for the voice of God.

I have also identified the church as a manifestation of the communion of saints—a community that honors and fosters sainthood in an era when sainthood is as important as it has ever been in human history but when it's not getting a lot of public credit. But all these things—our sacramental and incarnational heritage, our particular way of reading scripture, our focus on the community—are not things to brag about, not something we can claim credit for, but gifts. Or, to put it another way, even our virtues are gifts. They are things the Spirit has done in and with us. They are not badges of perfection or occasions of pride. As gifts, they are occasions for humble gratitude.

It shouldn't be hard for Anglicans to be humble. There is no more accidental form of Christianity than the one we have inherited. And I think this is another of our blessings. We are not the product of religious or theological zealotry, whether of a Tridentine or a Protestant sort. We have had no lack of deep and serious faith among us, but our Reformation was heavily determined by accident or, if you will, providence.

Henry VIII had a problem of conscience because he had married his brother's widow (which is forbidden in Leviticus 18:16). He had a problem of politics because he had not produced a male heir. And those two problems were further complicated by a personal dislike for any religion too different from what he had grown up with. The result was the English Reformation, an odd sort of experimental garden that yielded some surprising results.

Henry had to break with the Church of Rome in order to resolve his problems of politics and conscience. Yet, he was not ready to switch his allegiance to the continental forms of reformation. At his death, he left behind an unresolved theology and a church filled with tensions. His son and heir Edward VI (or at least the regents who had charge of him) tried to turn the matter in a more Calvinist direction. When he died young, his sister Mary I tried to push things in a Roman Catholic direction and might have succeeded had she not alienated the population with her violence.

Elizabeth I, the most important of Henry's offspring, came to the throne after a lifetime of being battered about by these changes in religious enthusiasm. Being the daughter of Henry's most Protestant wife, she was watched closely. She kept her head by keeping her mouth shut. What she wanted was a church where all her subjects could pray together. She was at least a competent theologian, but she wanted a church, not a theology factory in the Reformed style. She was, despite her intense pride and self-possession, a person of unusual humility in religious matters, prepared to allow a good deal of variation as long as everyone stayed in the family. If you decided you had to walk away in pursuit of your own religious purity and certainty, then you were on her bad list. But, even so, she did not get violent about such matters until the papacy began, in effect, to encourage efforts to assassinate her.

So we are the product of a historical jumble. And this is all right. It apparently gave the Spirit some room to work. I very much want to celebrate, praise, delight in, and advertise the wonderful gifts that I have received from God through the Anglican tradition. And I also want to remember that they did not emerge from our being great and wise and theologically perfect. We have had our moments of self-inflated pomposity, and sometimes we've have done real harm. But, at our best, we have managed to remember that we are not God, that we cannot pretend to match God's wisdom or love, that we are not and never will be able to speak God's mind with absolute certainty. This does not mean that we know nothing; it means that we remember that we are dust and to dust we shall return. And that translates pretty well to Rowan Greer's insight in describing the quintessentially Anglican stance as "a horror of absolutes and of infallibility."[32]

The classic term for this frame of mind is "humility," and humility is a tricky notion. Much of the time, we reduce it to groveling, to having a poor opinion of oneself. "The humble," in this usage, are those who are conscious only of their weakness and their failure. They would never think of speaking up or speaking out. They may have their own thoughts about matters, but who, after all, would care what they think? They will just fade back into the shadows and hope nobody even knows they're there. After all, the great sin is "pride," right? Thinking you *are* somebody. So the great virtue must be thinking you are nobody.

Thank God for the feminist writers of the last fifty years who have given this idea of humility a good beating. As they pointed out, humility of this sort can in fact be a serious sin. It allows people to sit back and disclaim all responsibility for the world around them with the excuse that it wasn't for *them* to do anything about it. The feminists were thinking about the long history of women in particular being admonished to cultivate humility—and being reproved when they seemed too assertive. But like all the great sins, it is really an equal opportunity corrupter.

Real humility is more complex. Consider the great scriptural exemplar of humility, Mary the Mother of Jesus. Her *Magnificat* begins this way:

> My soul doth magnify the Lord,
>   and my spirit hath rejoiced in God my Saviour.
> For he hath regarded
>   the *lowliness* of his handmaiden.
> For behold, from henceforth
>   all generations shall call me blessed.

For he that is mighty hath magnified me,
and holy is his Name.[33]

Mary was not only female, she was a poor nobody. So she doesn't speak lightly of "lowliness"; it was her everyday life experience. But she was not a doormat. She didn't have to say "yes" to God, and when she did, she knew what kind of chance she was taking. She knew she was doing something utterly bold. If she did not know it at the time, Simeon certainly told her bluntly that day in the Temple: "This child is destined for the falling and rising of many in Israel, ... and a sword will pierce your own soul, too" (Luke 2:34-35).

Mary knew about the distress of the world and cared about it. When she decided to take this profound risk, she was not merely being submissive. She was challenging God, like the psalmists and Job. Here's how I envision the moment:

She said, "Be it unto me
according to your word."
And the angel knelt, offering
as token of awe the one thing angels
have to sacrifice, their pride.

She offered what she could not know.
But she saw it was time
to risk, to dare the journey.
Tears are a certainty in every life.
What else lay beyond them?

What is striking in Mary's story is her realism. Her "lowliness" did not mean that she accepted passivity and helplessness. Indeed, she confidently expects God to turn it into greatness. She sees one thing that she can do and does it without worrying about the cost. And it turns out to be the critical choice.

Humility, then, is not self-abjection. It is actually very like sainthood—being willing for God's grace to shine through us for the world. Compare this prayer by Christina Rossetti:

I pray Thee, Lord Jesus Christ, make those whom
Thou lovest, and who return Thy love, mirrors of Thee
unto their unloving brethren; that these too becoming

enamoured of Thine image may reproduce it, light reflecting light, and ardour kindling ardour, until God
be all and in all. Amen.[34]

It is a particularly good prayer for the church right now—
this prayer that we might become mirrors of God's love,
"light reflecting light." It is a prayer of humility that also
boldly lays claim to a role in the transformation of the world,
not by asserting human will, but by reflecting grace onto one
another.

All of this is particularly relevant when we are talking
about the church because, of course, the church is always
struggling with it. Religion, we keep thinking, should be immune to the baser forms of human evil. That is why we get
incensed, outraged, or maybe depressed by the failures of the
church. It shouldn't be happening! And that's right, of course,
in an absolute sense.

But these failures are also, in some part, exactly what we
ought to expect. The gifts in which the church is so rich bring
out the best in us and also the worst. You may recall that
Jesus frequently attacked the religious leadership of his day.
He charged them with indifference toward those who suffered and toward people on the margins of society: "You tithe
mint and rue and herbs of all kinds, and neglect justice and
the love of God," he said to the religious authorities. "You
load people with burdens hard to bear, and you yourselves
do not lift a finger to ease them" (Luke 11:42, 46).

Often, we Christians have smugly imagined that Jesus was
denouncing *Judaism*. Not in the least. Judaism was just the
particular context in which Jesus encountered the problem.
Long before him, the prophets had denounced the religious
authorities of their day for the same reasons. And the same
faults are to be found in the church of every age.

Humility is the deep awareness that we are not God, not
even when we are speaking of God, teaching about God, celebrating God. We who profess religion are perennially
tempted to see ourselves as God's custodians. But the only
kind of God that has custodians is an idol.

It was the religious and the respectable who killed Jesus.
Oh yes, they enlisted the mob to do some of their dirty work.

But they were the instigators. Where does that leave religious and respectable people like us? I hope it leaves us with an awareness that we, too, are capable of turning against the God whom we thought we were serving, substituting our image of God, our codification of God, our practice of religion for the real God who cannot be possessed or confined. The Spirit blows where she likes. She is the eternal reminder that God will never be limited by any container we may construct. But that does not keep us from constructing them. And when we have our new idol all buffed and shining, we do not need to be *humble* any more. We've got it made! The great failure of religion is this tendency to make idols.

Let's devote a little attention, then, to some of our preferred forms of idolatry. Much of our Anglican idolatry has been specific to what one might call our "internal sectarianism." Since Anglicanism has never really been defined in terms of complete theological agreement, we have accommodated a variety of theological impulses, each of which has, at times, claimed special status and authority—and each of which is only part of a larger whole. Each of these has taken something of great value to all Anglicans and emphasized it to the point of downplaying some other things of equally great value.

Our old image of the three-legged stool of scripture, tradition, and reason may not be all that authoritative (or even helpful in resolving our conflicts), but it does a pretty good job of capturing the character of our internal sects. Evangelicals focus on scripture and show a strong Puritan heritage in the way they read it, not in terms of adhering to Calvin's trademark theological perspectives such as predestination, but in the assumption that scripture contains a clear, comprehensive, and decisive theological system. Liberals can be rather dismissive of both scripture and tradition because they get very focused on the present witness of reason. Anglican Catholics tend to look to tradition as the place where we get a comprehensive sense of what Christian faith is really all about.

Each of these sectarian impulses, of course, has given rise to a variety of interpretations and different ways of living it out. Each has its gifts and virtues, each its preferred idolatries.

77

Any brief account is certain to be full of elisions and miscon-
structions. But I am going to risk offering three rough
sketches anyway, because we have to begin thinking openly
together about these issues. Feel free to disagree with me all
you like, but think about these things.

Evangelicals

What are some of the gifts and virtues of evangelical Anglicanism? It has great enthusiasm for the word of God, the
scriptures. It has a zeal for encouraging a strong sense of personal relationship with God. It has been willing to encourage
a certain warmth of emotion that other Anglicans may be a
little squeamish about. It is capable of summoning people to
sacrificial living. In the past, Evangelicals have sometimes
shown great zeal against oppression. One thinks of the
Clapham Sect and its role in the abolition of the international
slave trade. On the other hand, in the nineteenth-century
United States, evangelical Anglicans were strong defenders of
slavery and there is still perhaps a certain tendency for Evangelicals to care more about individual morality than the well-
being of the larger society.

These are gifts that have made Anglicanism a richer tradition than it would otherwise have been. But, as I have been
suggesting, the icon can also become, with just a slight spin,
the idol. And we should probably expect to find the negatives
of Anglican Evangelicalism allied to its virtues.

One such problem is that Evangelicals often show an un-
necessary narrowness of spiritual vision. Rather than embracing the true breadth of scripture, they have tended to narrow
the spiritual path down to three steps: recognition that we
are rightly damned; acceptance that we are redeemed by
Christ's atoning sacrifice (usually interpreted in terms of the
doctrine of penal substitutionary atonement); and the embracing of a new life of sanctity. One can, in fact, find all this
in scripture—though the pedigree of the doctrine of penal
substitutionary atonement is pretty hazy; the problem is that
it leaves so much out. It seems to be a requirement, for example, that Evangelicals should reject the possibility that any
of the original blessing of creation could have survived the

fall. But the Bible is really not this systematic and to reduce all of Christian faith to a single formula excludes much of the ancient and medieval portion of the communion of saints, including some of our greatest spiritual writers. Indeed, it excludes too much of the Bible itself.

This, in turn, is really a special case of a larger problem in the evangelical world. The Calvinist/evangelical doctrine of the "plain sense" of scripture is tacitly taken to mean that this sense is, to all intents and purposes, now fully known. Indeed, the plain sense of scripture is essentially equated with evangelical theology. At worst, Evangelicals no longer return to the actual scriptures in their fullness, which are after all confusing and poorly organized and apt to mislead the public. It is easier simply to reiterate evangelical theology, prefaced by "As the Bible says...." A Baptist colleague of mine, who long taught at a major university in the American South, once told me that her students there had changed over the years. Once they had actually known the Bible fairly well, but as conservative Evangelicals increasingly dominated all Southern churches, her students proved increasingly ignorant even of the most basic and familiar passages. What they knew were just lists of proof texts that supported the doctrine of their home congregation.

I find that modern Anglican Evangelicals often refuse really to study scripture together with other Anglicans, and I see this as a great betrayal of their particular as well as our shared heritage. They keep saying, "The Bible says..." and insisting that this binds them. But in some cases, there is no breadth in their embrace of the scriptures and no real openness to them behind the claim. They seem to want the rest of us simply to take their word for what scripture says. This is not an expression of confidence either in God or in scripture. It is, I am afraid, an effort to protect an idol. The ruthlessness and dogmatism which have become hallmarks of contemporary evangelical leaders further bear this out.

I am trying to choose my words carefully here. Not every Evangelical, in or out of the Anglican Communion, is guilty in this respect. God has found lovers among the evangelical community; there are many people of grace and generosity there. Unfortunately, the loudest voices give Evangelicals the

public face I'm describing here. There are some quieter voices
that have something else to say, but they have not yet found
a broad audience. And it is difficult for them to speak up because one of the defining features of the contemporary evangelical movement seems to be its willingness immediately to
disown anyone who goes "off-message," who differs from
the official line. No surprises, please! The Bible is supposed
to behave itself.

Liberals

Now, if any reader is feeling singled out for attack here, I
would ask you to hang on a bit. I fully intend to be equally
unkind to everybody else—because these problems have to
be brought out into the open. If we allow ourselves to remain
locked into our sectarian idolatries, we shall quite rightly be
blown by the Spirit into the trash dump of dead sects.
Frankly, it is already getting full, as is the way with landfills.
I would rather see us engage in some recycling.

On, then, to liberal Anglicans. Again, there is much to be
said about the contributions these folk have made to our tradition as a whole. They have shown great respect for education and for contemporary thought. They have been willing
to engage with it, not just defend against it. They do not assume that people living in the fourth or the twelfth or the sixteenth century knew everything there is to know. They have
the courage to look around them and pay attention and think
new thoughts. If it weren't for liberals in the history of Christianity, we would have become completely paralyzed long
ago. The Nicene Creed, the vision of the Franciscans, the theology of Thomas Aquinas, the Reformation—you name it—
all the work of liberals, even if some of them later got turned
into conservative idols for the convenience of their successors.

Liberals have also displayed a strong critical faculty that
can cut through a lot of pretense and get rid of what no
longer serves the gospel. Bishop Jeremy Taylor was punished
for his rejection of the doctrine that unbaptized infants go to
hell, but it would be hard to find an Anglican today who
would not agree with him. The biblical scholar, mathemati-
cian, and missionary bishop John William Colenso looked

like a frightening radical in his own day when he published his Zulu dictionary and translated the scriptures into the Zulu language; he now looks like a prophet with his witness to the necessity for the gospel to become at home in every culture. Liberal Anglicans helped us deal with the nineteenth-century sea change in geology and biology and astronomy. Thinkers like F. D. Maurice helped us raise our sights toward a more ecumenical outlook. Liberals have stayed on the alert, decade after decade, to see what new questions are being raised about God and the meaning of the world. They have helped keep our voice from becoming stale and tedious.

At the same time, given their analytical and critical talent, liberal Anglicans sometimes forget the importance of broader and more positive approaches. I blame my own professional colleagues, the biblical scholars, among others. There have been distinguished exceptions; I need name only Austin Farrer or Reginald Fuller to make my point. But a great many Anglicans, including many clergy, think that biblical scholars exist only to tell them, "That's not what it means." It is as if we had washed our hands of responsibility for what it *does* mean. Admittedly, our failure is partly to do with the complexity of the task. But it has also been a backing away from our responsibility as members of the communion of saints.

Another form of this phenomenon is the sort of liberal Anglican who specializes in telling people what they don't need to believe any more. There is a real place for that. I have a close relative whose faith has been much strengthened by it. He grew up in a fundamentalist context, where the anger of God routinely eclipsed God's love. He could afford to shed a great deal of his childhood religion, and he still has plenty left to believe. But in itself, the message about what you *don't* have to believe does not help people build an intimate personal engagement with God. It may be one part of the good news of Jesus, but it is not the whole story.

Christians need the services of this kind of analytical and critical intellect. The problem arises when it turns into reductionism or when the cerebral, intellectual approach to faith is thought of as complete in itself. There is a danger of neglecting the fundamental insight that people are more than minds temporarily trapped in bodies. We are body, soul, and spirit. It is not enough to dismiss one's opponents as ignorant, as one hears done with some frequency. The most ignorant Christian in this world may have more faith than the best educated. God is no respecter of persons or of degrees.

Liberals can be as ruthless and dogmatic as Evangelicals. During our conflicts in the Episcopal Church over recent decades, I have listened to people from all sides complaining about mistreatment at the hands of others. I'm sure that, allowing for a certain amount of aggrieved enhancement, all the stories are broadly true. We have indeed gotten into the habit of passing summary judgments. But the really telling thing is that, if I say to those who are complaining, "Wait! Isn't this the same kind of thing that people in your group have been doing to those other folk whenever you happen to be in control?" they will not have any of that. They are not interested in anybody's suffering but their own, and that serves to reinforce their own determination to give no quarter. Liberals may embrace ruthlessness in a different form—"political correctness" rather than the "plain sense of scripture" or "the universal tradition of the church"—but the results are the same. One is confident of being always in the right.

Catholics

And now, let me come home to that part of our tradition to which I feel closest. I feel a deep debt of gratitude to catholic Anglicanism for giving me ancestors in the faith. I grew up in a denomination which, characteristically for American Christianity, had very little sense of its past. Good and faithful as those folk were and are, I felt like an orphan in the world— as if I had been left high and dry on some desert island with no notion how I'd gotten there. I had already read the Bible clear through a couple of times by the time I was twelve, and I loved it. But I could tell that its world was very remote. I had grandparents who could give me a sense of being in touch with pioneer days in Oklahoma. I loved the stories they told. But in terms of Christian faith, it was as if there was a kind of vacuum between AD 100 and AD 1950. I do remember one vacation Bible school when we were told a little about some early medieval saints—Martin and Boniface, if I remember correctly. I wanted more of that. And when I found myself in an Episcopal Church in my teens, I thought, "Oh, these folk are not strangers to this whole great story." I had found a history.

I also feel an immense gratitude for the tradition of music, poetry, and the arts that catholic Anglicanism has created and renewed and maintained, because it speaks to me along such a wide range of my humanity. I'm grateful for the catholic pioneers of the nineteenth century who brought back a fuller range of color and light and ceremony to Anglicanism. I'm grateful for the recovery of the monastic life. Even though I figured out in my early twenties that I wasn't cut out to be a monk, I have profited deeply by the contributions of the religious orders to our church's life. Catholics have continued to delve deeply into the mystery and meaning of the sacraments, and they partnered with other Christians in the Liturgical Movement and brought Anglicans in general toward a renewed sacramental focus.

So where are the problems? Some of it is a certain sense of entitlement. We see ourselves as allied with history, as the proprietors of tradition, as the default arbiters of authentic Anglicanism. We somehow thought we had the power of the veto. When you have thought for so long that you were history's friend and ally, it's a rude shock to wake up some morning and find the church's sense of the tradition's been moving off in another direction. I felt that way about the ordination of women in the beginning. "What's wrong with the way things have been? Why make changes at this late date? Why separate ourselves from two thousand years of our history?" Over time, I began to realize that I had given far too much credence to a definition of tradition that overstated its clarity and unchangingness. I had assumed that the tradition had a clear answer for everything. I had given it an authority that, by right, belongs to God alone. I had not entirely left the Spirit out of the equation, but I had given her pretty firm directions that she should confine herself to channeling grace through the sacraments and leave orthodoxy to the theologians.

She brought me my moment of enlightenment in an odd way. As a graduate student in early Christian literature, I was doing a lot of work on the Carthaginian church of the third century, the age of St. Cyprian. At one point I finally realized that this church—one of the pillars of early Western Catholicism—had actually been heretical. It rejected all baptisms performed by schismatics and heretics, even if they were in perfectly orthodox form, and required those so baptized to go through the rite again if they wanted to become part of the "great church." This is not the practice that eventually became the catholic consensus. In fact, it is the one embraced by the Donatist heretics. My first thought was, "How could this be?" My second thought was, "Oh! things have never been as tidy as I've wanted them."

Yet, the church at Carthage was not somehow invalidated by having been wrong on one point. It was still the church of martyrs and confessors that it had always been. Yes, its position on baptism contributed to more trouble down the line during the Donatist conflict, but no one can control the future. This is how I came to understand that the Episcopal Church would not cease to be catholic even if the ordaining of women turned out to be a mistake. I am grateful for that moment of understanding, because over the following years I began to meet women who were among the best priests, preachers, and pastors I have known. And I understood that the Spirit was indeed active among us in this regard for our good.

Catholic Anglicans sometimes make the same mistake in our treatment of the tradition that evangelical Anglicans make in their treatment of the scriptures. Rather than admitting the messiness and sometimes inconclusiveness of the past, we reduce this big, organic shrub that is our history to a simple diagram of one branch and say, "This is it. This is the real branch. It is perfectly formed. Forget all the rest." I liked that to begin with. I found it comforting. It took a lot of close study of Latin and Greek texts to convince me that it is not an option. This did not mean that tradition itself was meaningless. It just meant that I could not possess it in a tidy form that would guarantee I would always be in the right. Tradition is not a fossil, but a living being. And it lives in the communion of saints.

Catholic Anglicans have sometimes taken one historical element, one chapter or one page out of the tradition, and treated it as the compulsory pattern for Christian faith today. The nineteenth-century Cambridge Movement gravitated to the high Middle Ages, and catholic Anglicans wound up with some liturgical practices that came straight out of medieval court ceremonial. The Liturgical Movement of more recent times decided that, no, the model had to be the church of the fourth and fifth centuries. Well, with my enthusiasm for antiquity, I'm happy with that. But sometimes we have become so adamant about reproducing the model of another age, that we have not thought to look round and see exactly how it does or doesn't fit the very different world we are living in. I think, for example, of the way in which the Eucharist has become the principal Sunday service almost everywhere. Much as this suits my own preferences, I have discovered that some people who would just like to see what the Episcopal Church is like may avoid even peeking in the door because they are afraid they will feel as if they'll be pressed to make an immediate religious commitment: are you going to go forward or are you going to be the only person still sitting in the pew? Is the church welcoming to them or not? We have not yet thought this one through very well.

Idolatries

Now, I have tried to spread the offense pretty broadly here. And let me add that I have not particularly enjoyed it. For one thing, I believe that, at one point or another in my life, I have probably committed pretty much every sin I've just identified. This may be why I'm so conscious of them. I identify primarily with catholic Anglicanism. But I also have a strong connection with the liberal strand of Anglicanism—I am a New Testament scholar, after all. And I owe some of the key turns in my early growth in faith to evangelical writers, particularly to C. S. Lewis. I found a profound awareness of grace in his writings, especially his science fiction trilogy, the novel *Till We Have Faces,* and *The Great Divorce.* I also went through a powerful conversion in my early twenties, when I came to an intense realization that my plans for my own life

85

had gotten in the way of my trust in God. The outcome of that conversion was that things went on roughly as planned—but with a quite different me walking the path in a quite different spirit.

So, truth to tell, I have an ongoing love affair with all three of the internal sects that make up Anglicanism. I have received graces from God through all three. And I get angry at all three. I suppose I get angry partly because I can see myself fully capable of committing all those errors still. But I also get angry because I see our idolatries putting this great gift from God, the Anglican Communion, at risk.

One of the most destructive things about these idolatries is that they refuse to talk with one another. It would mean admitting that they are not God, after all, not the one true faith. True believers only really want to talk to themselves or to potential converts. Rather than converse with one another, we make pronouncements. Evangelicals will *tell* you what the scriptures say, because they have a lock on that. But don't expect to have any real conversation with them about it. Their job is to tell you; your job is to agree. Catholics *are* tradition; so of course we can't go into explanations about that. We just know we're right. Liberals have risen above all this old-fashioned and irrational stuff; so, no, they're not interested in what anybody else has to say.

No wonder there is so much anger evident among us. Having confessed to a share of it myself, I hope I may be allowed to bring forward a text of scripture that speaks quite directly to its peril in the context of church conflict:

> You must understand this, my beloved: let everyone be quick to listen, slow to speak, slow to anger; for your anger does not produce God's righteousness. (James 1:19–20)

It sounds like a spiritual diagnosis of exactly our situation, and indeed I suspect that the author was addressing some serious divisions in the church of his own time.[35] Anger is often the response of religious folk when our prejudgments are challenged. But there is even more to the text, an interesting element that is concealed in the New Revised Standard Version in the interests of generalizing the import of the passage.

The words translated "your anger" mean, more exactly, "the anger of an adult male." The Spirit has pinpointed one of our ongoing problems—the tendency of adult males to resort far too quickly to anger, which then threatens to poison any opportunity for faithful Christian conversation. Given the overwhelming dominance of men in the leadership of all our internal sects, particularly in their more rigid manifestations, this is an admonition not to be taken lightly. And note that it comes from an ancient patriarchal male who cannot be accused in any way of modern feminist perspectives.

Toward community

Deep down, our Anglican drive is not toward uniformity but toward community, toward worshipping together. Thank you, Elizabeth Tudor! If we can keep focused on that and keep inviting each other into the conversation, perhaps we can go forward together.

I want to commend three spiritual disciplines that can help us along. First, we need to reclaim that godly, comforting, and much neglected doctrine called "total depravity." This is not what you may be thinking. It does not mean that we are all rotten to the core and will never do anything right. It means rather that there is no moment in our lives, no place in our lives, where we are completely safe from turning good into evil. Nothing is completely safe, not even the church, not even religion—especially not religion.

Common use of the phrase "total depravity" is a good example of the thing itself. It is typically picked up as a stick to hit somebody by people who feel that they are pretty much immune to it themselves. Its very use involves a denial that it applies to *me*. So I want to rephrase it here slightly. Same doctrine, better formulation: "the total depravity of archbishops ...and everybody else." This may seem a bit depressing at first. But it's not a doom; it's just a danger. God can rescue us from it. If we remember that it's there, God may have an easier time rescuing us from it.

You see where this is going, I suspect. Being mindful of our own ability to turn toward evil is an incentive to practice humility. The one thing we can be quite sure of in life is that we are never going to be perfect. (And if you were, you'd be the last person to notice it.) But God can still use us. God can still do great things with us. The real God ... not our idolatrous substitutes.

So my first practical suggestion for cultivating humility is: *Treasure the doctrine of total depravity.* You have no idea how ingeniously you will live it out next. But, by God's grace, humility can return and tap you on the shoulder and call you back.

My second practical admonition is: *Treasure honesty.* We Anglicans have sometimes treasured politeness so highly that we lose our ability to speak the truth. I do not want us to lose what's left of our politeness—it's getting pretty frayed and careworn as it is. But I want us to learn to speak truth to one another, which is part of what I have been trying to do here. To do it well, of course, we also have to be prepared to listen when others tell us we are wrong. If humility and honesty can somehow get together, they will do much of the good work of politeness without embracing its more cowardly aspects.

Honesty allows the search for truth to enter public discourse and harness our hearts and minds together to its work. We try to express ourselves clearly. We invite others to do the same. If we disagree, we try to find the roots of the difference and look for perspectives that might reframe our differences. We challenge one another, not from a sense of infallibility, but in the desire to understand.

And my third practical admonition is: *Treasure the good news.* Look for it in your own words and in the words of others. If you are not hearing it at all, something has gone badly wrong. When the church gets focused so closely on conformity that it can ignore the human pain and need and hope and joy around it and within it, then the good news disappears. Look intently for it; listen for it everywhere. We have been through a drought of it, and we need a long drink of it. We can afford to drink deeply of it because, unlike water, it multiplies with the sharing of it. The most correct theology in the world is only an idol if we cannot hear it speaking good news to a world that needs it. What in our Anglican world here and now gives hope? What in our message strengthens love? What in our speech inspires trust in God? I have sat through a lot of church meetings where I didn't hear much of that. What I heard was pride, anger, idolatry.

So, cultivate humility. Speak honestly. Listen for good news. And then proceed boldly. We are the heirs of gifts whose value is beyond estimating. They are living gifts that have not even borne their finest fruits yet. And they live and grow by being shared.

If there are Anglicans who cannot join in this celebration of God's generosity, I grieve for that and want to keep any door I can open for them. But if there are some who, for the present, only want to repeat the shibboleths of their idolatry over and over and demand that others join them in the recitation, then we are not enslaved by their refusal of charity. It is enough that we remember our own fallibility. We practice humility. We speak honestly. We listen for good news and join in spreading it.

And we remember that the Spirit never gives up on her people. The good news of Jesus' incarnation is that it will indeed lead to the reflection and multiplication of love like light in a mirror.

I pray Thee, Lord Jesus Christ, make those whom Thou lovest, and who return Thy love, mirrors of Thee unto their unloving brethren; that these too becoming enamoured of Thine image may reproduce it, light reflecting light, and ardour kindling ardour, until God be all and in all. Amen.

6

JOINING IN THE SPIRIT'S
BUILDING PROJECT

O God of unchangeable power and eternal light: Look
favorably on your whole Church, that wonderful and
sacred mystery; by the effectual working of your providence, carry out in tranquillity the plan of salvation;
let the whole world see and know that things which
were cast down are being raised up, and things which
had grown old are being made new, and that all things
are being brought to their perfection by him through
whom all things were made, your Son Jesus Christ our
Lord; who lives and reigns with you, in the unity of
the Holy Spirit, one God, for ever and ever. *Amen.*[36]

This prayer for the church in the Good Friday liturgy speaks
directly to the necessity of change in human existence. While
the plan of salvation may look "tranquil" from God's perspective, it seldom does from the perspective of this world.
For us, it is a matter of believing that "things which were cast
down are... being raised up" and "things which had grown
old are ... being made new." It has happened over and over
again in the church's history. It is happening again now.

The gifts we have already received from the Spirit point
us forward. What are the two great sacraments about? They
are about the recreation of human community in the light of
Christ, brought to birth in the waters of baptism, fed with
God's own life in the Eucharist. What are the scriptures
about? They are the beginning chapters of God's continuing
pursuit of us in love and of our long struggle, in the commun-

ion of saints, to understand and respond in grace. What is the communion of saints? It is the seedbed, the experimental garden, of all that is best in our human potential. All these blessings have been shaping us for generations, centuries, millennia. And now, where might they lead us in the years to come? We can be sure there will be continuity. And we can be sure there will be surprises.

I began this reflection on the Anglican present and future with the Spirit's ability to shake up our familiar worlds and hurl us out in new directions. It happens time and again in scripture. Think, for example, of Philip the deacon (Acts 8). He was part of the Jerusalem church's Board of Seven, a group of people whose job was to make sure that the distribution of food to poorer members of the church was handled fairly, with no group being either preferred or neglected. In other words, he was an administrator. Probably he had some manifest talent for the work. Probably he liked it. Probably he expected to continue doing that job the rest of his life or until Jesus returned, whichever came first.

But then Stephen, another member of the Seven, was attacked by a mob and brought into court on heresy charges. He was convicted and executed. (You may recall that a young man named Saul helped out by watching the coats of the people who stoned him. Who could possibly have predicted how his story would turn out?) The attack on Stephen turned into a more general persecution that scattered most of the Christian community. Philip's administrative ministry evaporated, and he had to flee for his life. He wound up in some Samaritan towns. They were no doubt curious why he was on the run, and so he told them about the good news of Jesus. They caught his excitement and became the first non-Jewish group added to the church. What, in his life or temperament, had prepared him for this? The author of Acts doesn't tell us. Perhaps it was something Philip himself had never really noticed before.

In any case, he had just breached a major ethnic boundary, for, as we learn from the story of the Samaritan woman in John 4, Jews and Samaritans were so hostile to each other that they would not even drink from the same cup. Without intending to do anything new and without even the security of being able to consult anybody else, Philip had just set the church off into a new understanding of its mission. I say "Philip," but, of course, it wasn't just Philip. It was the Spirit who led him there, plopped him down in a strange place, and said, "See what you can do with this!" And he did something. The church bigwigs, of course, had to send a delegation along to make sure it was all right. But they came away persuaded that the Spirit was indeed at work.

That should have been enough for any one person's lifetime, but the Spirit had more in store for Philip. An angel tells him to go out and intercept a certain traveler on the Gaza Road. He turns out to be a eunuch who was a high official of the Queen of Ethiopia. He has been visiting Jerusalem and is now on his way home. The eunuch is reading from the prophet Isaiah and wondering what the passage means. Philip goes up to his chariot, gets into conversation with him, and, the next thing you know, he's baptizing him. None of this was in his plan. He would never have thought of trying such a thing. His ministry, the ministry he had loved and done so well, was to make sure that elderly widows got their dinner on time.

So, yes, there is always a lot that's new wherever the Spirit is at work. But not everything. Philip, after all, had encountered the Spirit before this. We do not know his whole story. But if he hadn't been a mature, trusted member of the Christian community, he would not have been appointed to the Seven. He had been baptized. He may have heard Jesus teach and seen some of his miracles; if not, he had heard the stories. He had been encountered by God in a variety of ways. He did not turn his back on all this when the Spirit sent him out on these unexpected errands. No, he took his previous experience with him. Once he had Samaritan converts—and then, amazingly, someone from faraway Ethiopia—he baptized them. He brought them into the continuing tradition of how the Spirit brings us life, and the mere addition of these strangers made the tradition new.

We, too, can assume that, as we move forward with the Spirit we will be taking our past experience with us. The One who met us before is the One who is still meeting us now. Not everything will go with us in exactly the form we knew it before. Philip's baptism probably took place in the setting of an existing Christian community. In Samaria, Philip was *creating* the Christian community with these new converts. At the baptism in the open desert near Gaza, it was just the two people, Philip and the eunuch—and probably a surprised audience of servants and guards. (He *was* a royal official, remember.) Still, Philip passed on the gifts he had been given, even though he had to improvise a new form for them. And he did not try to control everything in detail; he left matters, trustingly, in the hands of God.

The story ends quite strangely, as you recall. "The Spirit of the Lord snatched Philip away; the eunuch saw him no more, and went on his way rejoicing" (Acts 8:39). The eunuch didn't have Philip to rely on any more, but he wasn't abandoned. He went on his way rejoicing because he had come to trust in God in a new way and knew that the Spirit was with him, too.

Listening for the Spirit

So where do we start? A deep breath might not be a bad idea. The Spirit is the breath of God. The connection is not insignificant. When I was teaching introductory Greek to seminarians, some of whom were terrified of it, I learned that I had to remind them (especially during exams, but also in the middle of class sometimes) to breathe. Our mantra came to be, "The oxygenated brain is a happy brain." Yes, it was silly, but there is something very helpful about laughter, which is itself a form of breathing. Have you noticed that when something makes you laugh, it's hard to panic at the same time?

To breathe deeply—even to laugh—in the face of an uncertain future is an expression of faith, of trust in God. Nothing else will quite make up for it. You can be ever so serious and determined—all because you want to be faithful—and wind up thinking that everything is in your hands. Oh, such a mistake! The next step is usually panic—or the kind of rigid shutting down that is sometimes our defense against panic. But no, we each have a role to play—perhaps, like Philip, a number of roles—but we are not in charge. We need to breathe deeply and welcome the Spirit to our minds and hearts, to listen for what she is trying to convey to us. What she offers is seldom in the form of words. More often, it will be like artistic inspiration, images that give us just the nub around which we begin to create. And the Spirit spreads these inspirations around quite freely. Do not assume that you're safe from them because you are not clergy or not a lay leader. The Spirit picks on quite ordinary people, on the ordinariness in all of us.

So keep breathing and keep listening for the Spirit. And here are a few possible images that you may or may not find helpful. Very likely you will come up with better ones for your particular context. These are not programs to be executed; they are visions of possibilities. Philip could not have planned his response, either for the Samaritans or for the Ethiopian dignitary, in advance. What he received in the moment of opportunity was a vision of the church broader and more welcoming than anyone had hitherto thought of.

Image: the church as a community of repentance

"Oh, no," you're thinking; "we were hoping for a little encouragement here." Yes, exactly. What I mean is that the church is a community where you do not have to get everything right the first time. There is a kind of moralizing perversion of church life that turns it into a body of disapproving people who have never done anything wrong—or, more precisely, a body of disapproving people who pretend never to have done anything wrong and are hoping you do not find out about it. The true communion of saints understands that to be human is to err.

In a recent interview, the composer Arvo Pärt was talking about Estonian independence after the fall of the Soviet Union and the sometimes bitter emotions it aroused, when he broke off to say, "There is a good rule in spiritual life, which we all forget continually, ... that you must see more of your own sins than other people's. ... So I think everyone must say to himself, 'We must change our thinking.' We cannot see what is in the heart of another person. Maybe he is a holy man, and I can see only that he is wearing a wrong jacket."[37]

Turning loose of our pretense to perfect righteousness is a liberating experience. It is one of the things from which we religious people particularly need to be saved. The Columba who walked up and down Caledonia befriending strangers and telling people the good news of Jesus was the same Columba whose greed for learning had led to armed conflict and death. There was no way he could pretend to perfection. What he could do was repent and offer himself humbly to the use of the Spirit.

Repentance is really a way of consenting to grace. By recognizing all that we have done wrong when we tried to live without faith and hope and love, we can then accept the forgiveness that God is always eager to extend. By recognizing our need, we are enabled to return to the joyful heart. I refer to the joy that comes when we can fully and honestly acknowledge who we are and still have hope because God has claimed us and made us members of the communion of saints.

Repentance is a manifestation of the spiritual exercise recommended in the preceding chapter: the practice of humility, honesty, and attentiveness to the good news. Lack of trust in God makes us arrogant because it makes us fearful and lonely in this world. Lack of hope makes us cling to idols instead of risking life out in the open where God is at work. Lack of love, for self and others, fosters antagonism, quarrels, schism—all the many age-old afflictions of churches. Many years ago, I heard a sermon on the text "Love your neighbor as yourself." The preacher said, "I think, if we were to love our neighbors as we love ourselves, God help our neighbors!" There was a profound truth there. Much of our hatred of others is a thinly disguised mistrust and spite directed at ourselves.

The terrible works of fear, idolatry, and hatred threaten our whole world. We hear about them every day in the news reports. We cannot rescue the world from these evils. That is God's business. But we can begin to repent of them in our own lives and let the church, as communion of saints, become a kind of beacon, letting repentance shine as light in the dark around us. Repentance is not a dead end; it is a new beginning.

Image: the church as a community with deep roots

Perhaps this is an issue more among Americans than among Anglicans in other countries. Americans do tend to move away from our roots. I don't know how far back in my family's history you would have to go to find two generations living in the same place—at least the 1860s. We have our adaptations. We create new communities quickly in places that may not even have had houses ten years before. And we have a tradition of treating one's generational cohort as more important than one's family. But I have been seeing a certain sense among younger folk in the Bay Area of wanting to have a multigenerational community as well as the company of people their own age. This is not a flood, I hasten to add, but they are impressive folk. And, as I have already said about my own growing up, this sense of the church being a community with deep roots was something that drew me to the Anglican tradition.

Because we have problems about maintaining parishes in the face of demographic change and because we think we have to have new forms for a new day, there may be a tendency not to take notice of how rich and deeply rooted our church community can be. This includes the rooting of a congregation in a particular place and the rooting of the larger church in the whole story of scripture and our long ensuing history. In other words, I am talking once again about the communion of saints.

I do not mean to project a romanticized notion of the perfect community. That will only run afoul of reality. The community will still be full of human beings and therefore it will not be perfect. (See above: "doctrine of total depravity of archbishops, etc.") But the very deepest roots of this community are the law of love and the sacrifice of the cross and the universal call to live in Jesus' resurrection. At best, these make themselves felt in our life together; and, even at worst, they are still there, persistently raised up in our worship, to judge us and call us to repentance. We are not simply a group of people who happen to like one another or feel unthreatened by one another. We are the offspring of a rich past and the promise of a rich future.

Image: the church as a place of large welcome

Jesus got into trouble with the religious establishment because he associated freely with disreputable people and pushed his disciples to do the same. Naturally, once Jesus had ascended safely into the heavens, church life began exhibiting the tendencies of religious life in general. It made itself the sphere of the godly and reputable and looked down on the outsiders. Still, it remains capable of returning to Jesus' vision of a company in which very different sorts of people can come together in the love of God.

Our differences become a source of riches here. No one nation, era, class, or language can fully comprehend the love of God. God remains always a mystery, even when we think we know all there is to know. One of the most joyful things about church life in our multicultural time is the opportunity to see people from many different origins worshipping together in concord. It sometimes seems to happen most easily in places where there are many Anglican expatriates from different places. They find it easier to recognize one another as kin. In contrast, one of the saddest things about our current church divisions is that they threaten to reduce our diversity and, with it, our opportunity to understand God better through the eyes and hearts of Christians who may be quite unlike us.

And there is further to go. In every place, there are people who will not risk entering a church because they believe they will not be welcomed—because they are not perfect; because they are the "wrong" color; because they are gay, lesbian, transgendered; because they have never been there before and would not know how to behave.... It's a big step, whether from the inside or the outside, to cross the gap between Jew and Samaritan or to cross the road and talk with the foreign dignitary in the chariot.

Image: the church as a training camp for the love of God, self, and neighbor

This is a function that local congregations can fulfill extremely well for those who stick with them over the years.

But some of us need and want a faster version. This may be a particular need of the young, and we have often looked to institutions other than the parish for the purpose, for example to schools or to youth groups or to programs that give young adults a chance to devote a year or two to serving the world. When I call these "training camps," I am thinking of the military, which may not be a welcome image for some of my readers. I am a bit surprised to find myself using it. But I have observed younger relatives going away to what Americans call "boot camp" and returning with a new sense of what it means to belong to a community, to support and rely on the members of a team, to acknowledge the personal strengths of others and deal with their own strengths and weaknesses. I have seen them emerge with a new sense of self formed in the context of a community.

Whatever else is going on in any Christian community, the church is always about growth in faith, hope, and love. This is not something we are likely to learn in isolation from the challenges of real life. And it's not just a matter of head-learning, though that can be useful, too. It's a matter of rubbing up against a bunch of people who are, whatever our pretenses or our reservations, our strengths or weaknesses, committed to working with the law of love.

This is "experiential learning." Jesus' own teaching put it front and center. He juxtaposed, in the Twelve, people who were certain to dislike and disapprove of one another. Think, too, about the parables—how they never give you a straightforward story with a clear ending. They keep you off balance. Wait a minute! Who's the good person? Who's the bad person? Is it the prodigal son who finally came home? The elder brother who's too wedded to justice to learn love? The father who *isn't* after all being very fair, who doesn't even seem to think that's the main issue? What Jesus did so often was to push us toward self-knowledge and new possibilities by keeping us just enough off-center that we have to think afresh.

This is different from the church as a retreat or a refuge. A boot camp is a tough, demanding environment. One needs a real-world environment to learn in. And church apparently works for this purpose. A recent study of religion in the United States shows evidence that religious people are, on average, more civil than the non-religious and make better neighbors and citizens.[38] I don't think I expected that myself, but it makes sense. After all, we've done the boot camp.

Image: the church as a temple, a place where people can practice worship

You can fall into worship at any unpredictable time and place—on a walk in the woods, in the presence of great music, in unexpected moments when the love of God simply washes over you. But if you would like to *practice* worship, if you would like to have guidance in it and discover how to open yourself to it and make a regular pursuit of it, you need something a bit more predictable. Never absolutely predictable! God doesn't work that way. The church doesn't either. Sometimes we make worship rote, boring, flaky, trivial. But when we do it well—and we at least have a tradition of knowing how to do that—we manage to focus our gaze on the God who is always near, and worship follows even when we were hardly expecting it.

I am not thinking only of the high aesthetic levels that cathedrals and rich parishes can reach. I love our tradition of church music. I am deeply moved by a Gibbons motet or a Vaughan Williams hymn tune. But even under the simplest of conditions, our liturgy can find its balance. The essential thing is the way we have learned to focus together on the presence of God. It's not about the person who is leading worship. It's about the opportunity for everyone present to hallow God's name, to let our gratitude for God's gifts overflow, to let love respond to love.

Our world encourages us to race around and do many things at once. It doesn't encourage us to be still or focus. It doesn't give us much opportunity simply to *be*. A worshipping community can restore a truer perspective and do it in trust and hope and joy. The "beauty of holiness," of which we spoke earlier, is the key thing. And it can manifest itself in great splendor or in utter simplicity as long as we are clear about what we are doing.

Image: the church as a school with many levels

Jesus' way of teaching was parabolic. It keeps us off balance. And then it can be suddenly revelatory, as when you finally realize that you are the older brother unwilling to turn loose of even a small portion of your rights or when you fathom that the Samaritan approaching you by the roadside is a hereditary enemy who is about to turn himself into your neighbor. But even Jesus' teaching was no shortcut to learning how to be a human or a Christian. The communion of saints is also a vast project in continuing education.

There needs to be room for beginners. Many people in our world know almost nothing about Christian faith—or, worse, have taken on all sorts of misinformation, some of it from voices preaching hatred and repression as if they were gospel. Newcomers need not indoctrination, but help in discovering the good news and thinking about it in relation to their own lives.

We also need refresher courses for the old hands. There needs to be opportunity for digging deeper into our experience of God in company with one another and with the help of the scriptures and the great tradition of the saints. As I look back over my earlier life, I realize I had to do too much of this with the help of long-dead writers, whose works I was fortunate to come across. I am glad to see that we have more opportunities to work together face-to-face now. But we are still not doing everything that would be desirable. Every sermon is an opportunity to further this process, but sermons are probably not enough by themselves.

Image: the church as a treasure house of the spiritual arts

I am thinking here partly about our heritage from the past: the poets, the painters, the composers, the architects. These are saints who have given life and hope to all sorts of people, including some outsiders who could not find it in the regular life of the church. We should be happy to share them in any way possible.

At the same time, we aren't just an archive for preserving relics. We are or should be an art institute, committed to preserving the old as a way of encouraging the new arts of the spirit. One thing about art is that it requires a certain freedom of the imagination. Art is not the same thing as theological thinking, and if we get too nervous about whether it's toeing the official line, we will wind up stifling it. I think, for example, of C. S. Lewis's little book *The Great Divorce,* where he used the wonderful device of programming regular bus service between hell and heaven. I am sure there were and are theological critics who were disturbed by his lapse of orthodoxy, but he succeeded in allowing some of us to think of both heaven and hell in quite different and more compelling ways—ways that actually illuminated life here and now.

Image: the church as a banqueting house

I draw this image from the Song of Songs: "He brought me to the banqueting house, and his intention toward me was love" (2:4). The banqueting house is where the lovers meet to delight in food and song. Here God gathers all God's beloved to delight in the love of God and of one another. It is the great feast on the mountain spoken of in Isaiah 25. It comes close to us in the eucharistic assembly. It is known in the service of feeding the poor. It can emerge in the companionship of coffee hours and church suppers.

Think about how much energy goes into describing the provision of food in the scriptures. God creates the plants for human sustenance. God gives permission to Noah and his descendants to eat meat as well. Wisdom prepares her feast and goes out to invite her guests. When there is nothing for David and his men to eat, the priest gives them the consecrated loaves. Jesus provides wine for the wedding feast and bread in the wilderness. He would not make a loaf for himself when the devil tempted him, but he multiplied loaves so that everyone could eat. And one great image of the age to come is the marriage supper of the Lamb.

The church should be celebrating food, not only in the fellowship of eating together, but in the art and craft of producing it and bringing it to the table. This may be pertinent in a new way at a time when an urbanized world is rediscovering that a connection to the earth is vital to human life and well-being. There is a great opportunity to reclaim a faithful relationship with the larger creation by getting reconnected with the sources of our sustenance.

Image: the church as the place where mercy and truth actually meet together

This meeting isn't easy to manage. We think of truth as unyielding and indifferent. We think of mercy as personal and gracious and creating new possibilities. We tend to view them in terms of "one or the other," not "both/and." Those of us who want to be lovers of truth accuse other Christians of being spineless pushovers. Those of us who want to be lovers of mercy accuse other Christians of being harsh and inhumane. We sometimes feel as if we would *like* to be rid of each other. But that is not what God is trying to create among us. As the psalmist wrote,

> I will hearken what the LORD God will say;
>> for he shall speak peace unto his people,
>>> and to his saints,
>> that they turn not again unto foolishness.
>
> For his salvation is nigh them that fear him;
>> that glory may dwell in our land.
>
> Mercy and truth are met together:
>> righteousness and peace have kissed each other.
>
> Truth shall flourish out of the earth,
>> and righteousness hath looked down from heaven.
>>> (Ps. 85:8–11)[39]

Christina Rossetti notes a parallel tension in *The Face of the Deep*. She cites a verse from Revelation, "He said unto me, Write: for these words are true and faithful" (Rev. 21:5b), and then she continues: "*True* is isolated, absolute, self-sufficient: *faithful* is relative, tenderly considerate. True is an announcement: faithful a promise."[40] There is a whole world of theology and spirituality here. What kind of church can we wish to be—what sort of church would it be *worth* being—without both of these, without truth *and* faithfulness, truth *and* mercy?

Image: the church as humanity participating in the vast community of creation

There has been a good deal of conversation over the last few decades about how the churches can behave responsibly in the light of the growing ecological crisis of the world. I am certainly in favor of churches behaving responsibly; it's a matter of good citizenship if nothing else. And we have gone on to assign it a theological and spiritual interpretation as stewardship of the earth. That's a start.

But something more is necessary. We do not really read the first creation story in Genesis carefully. We just hurry ahead to the point of *difference: we* are made in the image of God; *we* are in charge. Talk about taking the text out of context! No, the first great motions of creation have to do with beings far larger and more powerful than we: the sea, the land, the heavens and the heavenly bodies. The earth had a rich population of animals before the naked two-legged ape joined them. And God did not say of the animals, "This is good, but it could be better." Or, "This is good, but it needs something else." Or, "This is good, but what I'd really like is to see some little miniatures of myself running around in it." No, it was just *good.* When it was all done, it was *very* good. But if we drive ourselves out of existence, God will still be able to look at the world as it rebuilds without us and say, "This is good."

We could use a big dose of humility when we start thinking about our role in the world and in God's plan for it. We are, after all, creatures like all the rest. Some of them, like the mountains and the great whales, are much grander and more powerful than we. Some of them, like the angels, are more finely tuned intellects. Many of them are more beautiful. Some of them are tiny and yet change the fate of nations. Think of the tsetse fly or the *Anopheles* mosquito or, smaller yet, the pathogens they carry. In this great efflorescence of creation, we are just one part, a part that seems to have gotten out of hand.

Part of the remedy is to work hard together on reining in our destructiveness. But another, deeper part of it is to regain a due sense of proportion—a sense of reality to prompt and guide this work. And, so, whatever else the Spirit is calling us to, I believe she is calling us to resume a creaturely place in the world. As I have already suggested, the scriptures give us cues for this. Think of the words of Psalm 104, praising God for the alternation of night and day:

> Thou makest darkness that it may be night;
>   wherein all the beasts of the forest do move.
>
> The lions, roaring after their prey,
>   do seek their meat from God.
>
> The sun ariseth, and they get them away together,
>   and lay them down in their dens.
>
> Man goeth forth to his work, and to his labour,
>   until the evening.
>
> O LORD, how manifold are thy works!
>   in wisdom hast thou made them all;
>   the earth is full of thy riches. (Ps. 104:20–24)[41]

We are part of this great creation. We are not separated from it, not set over against it.

Christina Rossetti celebrated the world as a community of praise for the Creator in a poem entitled "'To what purpose is this waste?'"[42] which you will probably recognize as the disciples' complaint about the ointment a woman used to anoint Jesus at the house of Simon the leper (Matt. 26:8). It begins in just that frame of mind. She has gone walking in the countryside on "a pleasant day in June," but, like a good Victorian entrepreneur, she begins to think what a shame it is that all this open space is serving no human *use*. Drowsy, she lies down to nap:

> ...I sought out a place
> For rest beneath a tree,
> And very soon forgot myself in sleep:
> Not so mine own words had forgotten me.
> Mine eyes were opened to behold
> All hidden things,
> And mine ears heard all secret whisperings:
> So my proud tongue that had been bold

To carp and to reprove,
Was silenced by the force of utter Love.

She has a dream-vision of the complex inter-relatedness of
nature, little of which has any direct reference to humanity,
nor does it need any human justification:

A lily blossoming unseen
Holds honey in its silver cup
Whereon a bee may sup,
Till being full she takes the rest
And stores it in her waxen nest....

. . . . . .

And other eyes than our's
Were made to look on flowers,
Eyes of small birds and insects small:
The deep sun-blushing rose
Round which the prickles close
Opens her bosom to them all.
The tiniest living thing
That soars on feathered wing,
Or crawls among the long grass out of sight,
Has just as good a right
To its appointed portion of delight
As any King.

Our failure of vision, she recognizes, is like the disciples' failure to recognize the value of the anointing of Jesus. The value
of that extravagant act lay in its celebration of love and creation.

We want the faith that hath not seen
Indeed, but hath believed His truth
Who witnessed that His work was good:
So we pass cold to age from youth.
Alas for us: for we have heard
And known, but have not understood.

O earth, earth, earth, thou yet shalt bow
Who art so fair and lifted up,
Thou yet shalt drain the bitter cup.

Men's eyes that wait upon thee now,
All eyes shall see thee lost and mean,
Exposed and valued at thy worth,
While thou shalt stand ashamed and dumb.—
Ah, when the Son of Man shall come,
Shall He find faith upon the earth?

If we refuse to join in the worship offered by creation as a whole, says Rossetti, we are without faith ourselves and will end by violating the earth. She seems to have been looking into the realities of our time as well as her own. Our modern carelessness about the earth challenges not merely our physical survival, but our spiritual survival. We need to rediscover how central the whole created order is to our own faith. Will Jesus, returning, find that we have kept faith with the creation and the creator? And how would we keep faith with the one unless we keep faith with the other? We can yet become a more faithful sort of church if we learn to join in the song of creation in this way.

The Holy Spirit is clearing her site. She is digging her foundations. She sometimes resorts to heavy equipment for this, but mostly she tends to favor handtools and labor-intensive methods. She is an artisan at heart. This means that she is looking for a lot of assistants. And she deals out tools, skills, advice, encouragement, reproof if necessary.... She is the Spirit of truth and the Spirit of mercy and faithfulness. She is the Spirit of prophecy. She is the Spirit of contemplation and understanding. She is the Spirit of inquiry and wisdom. She is the Spirit of hospitality and grace. She is the Spirit of hope—perhaps especially, in our time, of hope. Church people have often looked disheartened in recent years. We need hope in a way that we cannot even measure. And the Spirit is eager to lead us toward it—to help us, like Hagar, to find the spring in the desert (Gen. 21:15–19).

She will invite you into the task. I spoke earlier about Philip and how the Spirit sent him here and sent him there and showed him how to break down barriers. Most of us are not going to be in Philip's exact predicament, swept away from our secure world by persecution or other disaster or even by the direct action of the Spirit, picking us up and snatching us away. No, we are going to stay pretty much where we are. But, with the Spirit's help, we are going to see the place anew. We are going to see ourselves anew, too. We are going to recognize our gifts and, in humility and hope, we are going to become agents of a holy beauty that we do not yet fully understand.

Do not be alarmed if there are moments that are perplexing and difficult. It isn't easy for God to get through to us. We do not understand God's language. God knows how to speak ours, but it can be difficult to say everything God wants to say in Hebrew or Greek or English or whatever. And besides that, the airwaves and the Web are so full of static and gabble and spam. So are our own minds and hearts and souls! But if we keep listening, the good news will make its way through. And the Spirit will lead us forward.

O God of unchangeable power and eternal light: Look favorably on your whole Church, that wonderful and sacred mystery; by the effectual working of your providence, carry out in tranquillity the plan of salvation; let the whole world see and know that things which were cast down are being raised up, and things which had grown old are being made new, and that all things are being brought to their perfection by him through whom all things were made, your Son Jesus Christ our Lord; who lives and reigns with you, in the unity of the Holy Spirit, one God, for ever and ever. *Amen.*

ENDNOTES

1. David F. Holland, *Sacred Borders: Continuing Revelation and Canonical Restraint in Early America* (New York: Oxford University Press, 2011), 18–20.

2. Christina Georgina Rossetti, *The Face of the Deep: A Devotional Commentary on the Apocalypse* (London: SPCK, 1892), 115.

3. English translations of the Bible have historically used masculine pronouns to refer to the Spirit. The equivalent terms in Hebrew and Aramaic, however, are feminine and the Greek term is neuter in gender. English practice must have derived from the influence of the Latin *spiritus,* which is masculine. When not quoting scripture, I will follow the Semitic usage and employ feminine pronouns.

4. See the "Introduction" by Betty S. Flowers in Christina Rossetti, *The Complete Poems,* ed. R. W. Crump (London: Penguin, 2001), xliv. See also Frances Thomas, *Christina Rossetti* (Hanley Swan, Worcs.: The Self-Publishing Association with Frances Thomas, 1992), 13–15, 42–43, 100–101. Dorothy Margaret Stuart sees Rossetti's resistance to the Roman Church as owing something to other family influences, particularly her mother's faith and the Pre-Raphaelite Brotherhood's lack of interest in the movement toward Rome; see Stuart's *Christina Rossetti* (London: Macmillan and Co., 1930), 142–44.

5. Rossetti, "Cardinal Newman," *The Complete Poems,* 584–85.

6. Robert D. Putnam and David E. Campbell, with Shaylyn Romney Garrett, *American Grace: How Religion Divides and Unites Us* (New York: Simon & Schuster, 2010), 120–133.

7. Rossetti, *The Face of the Deep,* 543.

8. For a fuller exposition of this understanding of priesthood, see L. William Countryman, *Living on the Border of the Holy: Renewing the Priesthood of All* (Harrisburg: Morehouse Publishing, 1999), 3–46.

9. Rosemary Dobson, "The Edge," in Les A. Murray, ed., *Anthology of Australian Religious Poetry* (North Blackburn, Victoria: CollinsDove, 1986), 157. Used by arrangement with Rosemary Dobson, c/o Curtis Brown (Aust) Pty Ltd.

10. William Temple, *Christian Faith and Life* (New York: Macmillan, 1931), 67–71.

11. Henry Vaughan, "The Night," in *Henry Vaughan: The Complete Poems,* ed. Alan Rudrum (New Haven: Yale University Press, 1976), 289–90; ll. 49–52.

12. The painting belongs to the Philadelphia Academy of the Fine Arts. For an image and discussion, see Dewey F. Mosby, Darrell Sewell, and Rae Alexander-Minter, *Henry Ossawa Tanner* (Philadelphia: Philadelphia Museum of Art, [1991]), 168–71.

13. Marcia Falk, trans., *The Song of Songs: Love Lyrics from the Bible* (San Francisco: HarperSanFrancisco, 1993).

14. Ariel Bloch and Chana Bloch, trans., *The Song of Songs: The World's First Great Love Poem* (New York: Random House, 1995).

15. Henry Vaughan, "The Revival," in *Henry Vaughan: The Complete Poems,* 370.

16. Thomas Traherne, "The Bible," in *Thomas Traherne: Selected Poems and Prose,* ed. Alan Bradford (London: Penguin Books, 1991), 103.

17. The painting is in the Kimbell Art Museum, Fort Worth, Texas.

18. This topic is further developed in my *Love Human and Divine: Reflections on Love, Sexuality, and Friendship* (Harrisburg: Morehouse Publishing, 2005).

19. My thanks to Australian friends who made me aware of the series of paintings *Christ in the Wilderness* by Stanley Spencer, which are now in the Art Gallery of Western Australia. They are the only examples of this theme I have come across.

20. A prayer "For Quiet Confidence," in *The Book of Common Prayer* (New York: Church Hymnal Corporation, 1979), 832.

21. *The Book of Common Prayer* (New York: Oxford University Press, 1928), 363.

22. These are the Daily Office lessons for the Friday of Proper 24, Year Two, according to the calendar in the 1979 *Book of Common Prayer,* page 989. It would be unusual to have all three of the readings at one service; the norm would be to divide them between Morning and Evening Prayer, with the addition of Psalm 35 for Evening Prayer.

23. W. H. Auden, *Collected Poems,* ed. Edward Mendelson (New York: Random House, 1976), 289.

24. Christian Jarrett, "Religion Causes a Chronic Biasing of Visual Attention," Research Digest blog of the British Psychological Society, September 16, 2010; found at http://bps-research-digest.blogspot.com/2010/09/religion-causes-chronic-biasing-of.html.

25. *The Book of Common Prayer* (1979), Collect for All Saints' Day, 245.

26. *The Hymnal 1982* (New York: Church Hymnal Corporation, 1985), hymn 423.

27. Gerard Manley Hopkins, "God's Grandeur," in *The Poems of Gerard Manley Hopkins,* ed. W. H. Gardner and N. H. MacKenzie, fourth edition (London: Oxford University Press, 1970), 66.

28. *The Book of Common Prayer* (1928), 467.

29. *The Book of Common Prayer* (1979), 47–48.

30. *The Hymnal 1982,* hymn 293; words by Lesbia Scott.

31. L. William Countryman, "The Disciples," in *Lovesongs and Reproaches: Passionate Conversations with God* (Harrisburg: Morehouse Publishing, 2010), 120–21.

32. Rowan A. Greer, *Anglican Approaches to Scripture: From the Reformation to the Present* (New York: Herder & Herder, 2006), 152.

33. *The Book of Common Prayer* (1979), 65.

34. Rossetti, *The Face of the Deep,* 115.

35. L. William Countryman, *Interpreting the Truth: Changing the Paradigm of Biblical Studies* (Harrisburg: Trinity Press International, 2003), 117–27.

36. *The Book of Common Prayer* (1979), 280.

37. Arthur Lubow, "The Sound of Spirit," *The New York Times Magazine,* October 17, 2010, p. 36.

38. Putnam and Campbell, *American Grace,* 443–92.

39. *The Book of Common Prayer* (1928), 446.

40. Rossetti, *The Face of the Deep,* 487.

41. *The Book of Common Prayer* (1928), 468–69.

42. Rossetti, "'To what purpose is this waste?'" in *The Complete Poems,* 740–44.